PLAYING POTUS

PLAYING POTUS

The Power of America's 'Acting Presidents'

PETER FUNT

Jefferson Bay Books

Hardcover ISBN: 978-1-7376267-2-5
Paperback ISBN: 978-1-7376267-3-2

Printed in the United States

First Hardcover Edition: June 2023

Please direct inquiries regarding excerpts from this book,
video clips or interviews to: Media@CandidCamera.com.

More information: www.PlayingPOTUS.com

About the cover

During his time on "Saturday Night Live," Phil Hartman, the acclaimed presidential impersonator best remembered for his Bill Clinton character, cheerfully accepted the nickname Mr. Potato Head. "When you're so average looking," he said in an interview with NBC's Bob Costas, "when they put a wig on you and some glasses, if you alter your face and your voice in any way, you can look a lot different."

Hartman's moniker prompted my request to artist Howard McWilliam ("McBill"), whose clever images appear often in *The Week* magazine, for a Mr. Potato Head cover.

The hair and necktie are Trump's, the aviator glasses Biden's, the ears are Obama's, the nose Clinton's and the mouth Carter's. One hand makes Clinton's thumbs up, while the other does Nixon's "V" sign.

Dedication

Though I hope that in some small ways I have provided inspiration to my children, Stephanie and Danny, it is often they who inspire me.

Steph is a public interest attorney, devoted to helping society's neediest members. Danny is a journalist, passionate about the kind of reporting and storytelling that is both informative and entertaining.

I'm proud to dedicate this book to them.

CONTENTS

The acronym POTUS has been in use since 1894, when it was adopted as code by telegraph operators who didn't wish to tap out "President of the United States."

Foreword

THE ONLY PERSON I've ever imitated with any success was my math teacher, Mr. Robert. I did his voice fairly well—a monotone, apparently from somewhere in the Midwest. But the key to my impression, a *hook* as comedians call it, was Mr. Robert's excessive and often misplaced use of the word "what." He constantly asked the class questions and then, without pausing, answered them himself. His best utterance, never to be forgotten by those in geometry class, came after he drew lines on the blackboard and said, "These lines are perpen- what? Dicular!"

The fact that I wasn't good at either geometry or imitations didn't diminish my interest in entertainers who did impressions on record albums and television. I was particularly intrigued by political routines, the kind done in my youth by breakthrough artists Vaughn Meader (JFK), David Frye and John Byner (LBJ) and Rich Little (Nixon). I was able to interview Little and Byner for this book. Meader died in 2004, but I did speak at length with his producer. Though Frye died in 2011, I learned a lot about him from his sister.

Another benchmark for this project came during the 2008 presidential campaign when I wrote a piece for *The Washington Post* about how a fictional presidential candidate had served a few years earlier as a calculated test for Barack

Obama's presidential run. Writers of the Emmy-winning drama "The West Wing" created a character named Matt Santos (played by Jimmy Smits) who becomes America's first nonwhite president. Working with Obama's chief strategist, David Axelrod, writer Eli Attie created the Santos character based on Obama. "We were trying to look at what was happening in the country and around the world," Attie told me. "Things are more multicultural, more diverse. We tried to look ahead of the curve, and it seemed inevitable that a successful Latino or black candidate would emerge." Even though Obama had not yet won his Senate seat, Axelrod was promoting him as "handsome, appealing, articulate"—a politician who could find new paths to solve old problems; a minority candidate who could show pride in his race without allowing it to define him. That's what Matt Santos became. When Obama was elected president, Axelrod emailed Attie to say, "We're living your script." For me, it seemed remarkable that politics could imitate art.

During 2019 and 2020 I spent much time on the road in Iowa, Nevada and California, writing columns about the Democratic presidential candidates for *USA Today* and *The Wall Street Journal.* I watched Joe Biden, Bernie Sanders, Amy Klobuchar, Pete Buttigieg and others at close range, then studied how these politicians were being portrayed on "Saturday Night Live." Rachel Dratch's Klobuchar, Colin Jost's Buttigieg and Larry David's Sanders deserved a lot of votes.

I wrote a *USA Today* column examining the controversy caused by Jim Carrey's portrayal of Biden on SNL. Some Democrats thought Carrey's character was too negative and could hurt Biden's chances at the polls.

The question of to what extent political impressionists influence public opinion became central in developing this book. I also turned up fascinating backstories for the performers and writers who, since the early '60s, invented and gradually modified the art of imitating sitting presidents via mass media.

I'm reminded of what Kurt Vonnegut wrote as the thesis for his novel "Mother Night":

"We are what we pretend to be, so we must be careful about what we pretend to be."

Peter Funt
Pebble Beach, California

1 / *Mimics*

O
n the night of January 4, 1928, the most acclaimed comic of the day, Will Rogers, participated in a landmark radio program linking entertainers from around the country in a live broadcast, requiring 20,000 miles of wire to create the hookup. Speaking from his Beverly Hills home, Rogers began with his trademark blend of sarcasm and corn: "All the movie stars out here are making New Year's resolutions and taking new wives. It's a question which they're going to drop first." After a bit more banter Rogers told listeners of "a great surprise" and went on to say, "I want to introduce our President to you, Cal Coolidge." Using what a reporter for *The New York Times* described as "the nasal twang of the President," Rogers imitated Coolidge, even tossing in a plug for the program's sponsor. "It gives me great pleasure to appear before you through the courtesy of Dodge Brothers and report on the state of the nation as a whole. You know, the nation is in a hole, but I think that the nation is perfectly all right."

The following day letters and telephone messages arrived at the White House from listeners who were troubled by the routine. According to coverage in *The Times*, "Mr. Rogers

Will Rogers

did not directly explain that this was a 'joke' and some persons seemed to have thought the President was speaking in behalf of the new Dodge car. In this, some of those close to the President thought today that Mr. Rogers exceeded good taste." Rogers took a cue from the coverage and apologized in a letter to the White House, for "my lack of good taste, or utter stupidity."

President Coolidge, who reportedly had not heard the broadcast, wrote back to Rogers: "I hope it will cheer you up to know that I thought the matter of rather small consequence myself though the office was informed from several sources that I had been on the air. I wish to assure you that your note makes it all plain that you had no intention save harmless amusement." However, years later reports surfaced that Coolidge had, in fact, eavesdropped on the 1928 broadcast and was annoyed.

◆ ◆ ◆

EVERY U.S. PRESIDENT has been portrayed by an actor in film or on TV. Joseph Kilgour played George Washington in a batch of silent films in the early 20th century; others playing Washington over the years include Jon Voight, Peter Graves, Adam West, Jeff Daniels and Kelsey Grammer. Abe Lincoln is among the most popular presidents to be played on screen, with actors including Walter Huston, Henry Fonda, Gregory Peck, Hal Holbrook, F. Murray Abraham and Sam Waterston stepping into the role before being overshadowed by Daniel Day-Lewis's Oscar-winning performance in the 2012 Steven Spielberg biopic "Lincoln." But only since 1962—with rare exceptions, such as the brief Will Rogers episode—have presidents been played by actors and comedians while in office.

During Herbert Hoover's term, radio impressionists—or "mimics" as they were known in the day—occasionally filled more serious roles. A weekly news series launched in 1931, "The March of Time," used actors to deliver reenactments, often including presidential dialogue. Ted di Corsia provided the voice of Hoover, followed by William Adams as Franklin Roosevelt. It's worth noting that until FDR began his fireside radio chats in 1933, most Americans had never heard the sound of their president's voice. (The first radio message by a president was Warren Harding's in 1925). The Roosevelt Administration persuaded broadcast networks to ban impressions of the president, except in serious news recreations—and even then, producers of "The March of Time" were required to obtain specific permission to use a Roosevelt sound-alike.

Concern about the role of mimics on radio came to a

head in 1937 when a performer named Arthur Boran was cut off the air by New York City station WMCA as he imitated Roosevelt during a press banquet in Albany. "We ban presidential imitators," stated WMCA's Larry Nixon, "because too many in the unseen audience might think it was actually Mr. Roosevelt at the microphone, whether the mimic delivers a serious speech or mere nonsense. Furthermore, mimicking is not good broadcast entertainment and by eliminating it we protect the listener from confusion."

While Roosevelt and his aides worked to limit presidential mimicking in public, FDR had a fondness for the genre in private. He developed a relationship with the actor Dean Murphy, who did brief impressions of both Franklin and Eleanor Roosevelt in the 1944 film "Broadway Rhythm." Murphy reportedly made at least 17 appearances at the White House, doing FDR's

Dean Murphy, on the cover of Billboard Magazine.

voice for the President and his guests, once receiving a pair of ruby cufflinks as a gift. Roosevelt also autographed a photo with the words, "To Dean Murphy who looks more like Franklin D. Roosevelt than I do." Unfortunately there doesn't seem to be any audio or visual record of Murphy's White House performances. Matthew Hanson, archivist at the Roosevelt Library in Hyde Park, N.Y., explained in an email, "We don't have that, and I'm not aware of another repository who would. Entertainment at the White House was typically not recorded. Also, there was not yet a White House photographer as there has been with more modern presidents."

"The March of Time" ended its radio run in 1945, just as Harry Truman took office. Truman and his successor, Dwight Eisenhower, were heard often on radio and gradually on TV, ending the need for mimics. Meanwhile, the strain of World War II eliminated most, if not all, attempts at comedic presidential impersonations.

◆ ◆ ◆

FOR JOHN F. KENNEDY, a Beltway observer once noted, television press conferences functioned much like Twitter does today—providing unfiltered communication between the president and the public. Kennedy held history's first live televised presidential press event on January 25, 1961, just five days after taking office. As he learned months earlier in debating Richard Nixon, his affable style and youthful vig-ah played well on TV. By the time of his death in 1963, JFK had held 64 news conferences, an average of one every 16 days, opening the door for impressionists. Audiences were, in effect, pre-conditioned by Kennedy

himself to accept comic portrayals that burst onto the scene—
particularly those using a mock Q&A format.

At a New York City club on Fourth Street known as Square
East, in the winter of 1962, members of the acclaimed Second
City troupe performed a nightly political revue that included
improv answers to audience questions. The characters were
John Kennedy and Soviet Premier Nikita Khrushchev, played by
Andrew Duncan and Eugene Troobnick. Asked at one perfor-
mance about the Berlin crisis, Duncan said, "We must not run
in fear, but on the other hand we must not fear to run." Although
performed without costumes or props, the impersonations
resonated with patrons. A similar sketch was also popular at
Second City's home in Chicago, with Roger Bowen as JFK and
Alan Arkin as Khrushchev...

> Q: *Would Mr. Kennedy comment on the slogan "Better
> Red than Dead?"*
> KENNEDY: *These are obviously both extreme positions.
> I have tried to keep my government on the solid middle
> road between them. That is to say—half dead and half
> Red.*
> Q: *What will Mr. Krushchev say at the next disarmament
> conference?*
> KRUSHCHEV: *We in the Soviet Union believe that total
> disarmament is necessary for peace. We are always for
> peace. Anybody who stands in the way of peace will be
> destroyed.*

A Kennedy press conference routine was also being
developed by the actor-writer Elliott Reid who, in addition to

several movie roles, had worked as an impressionist, with a focus on politics. When he was just 15, during the Roosevelt Administration, Reid landed a radio role on "The March of Time." Twenty-seven years later, a family connection at *Time* magazine helped him get an invitation to entertain at the '62 White House Correspondents' Dinner, alongside President Kennedy. In a letter shared with me by his nephew, Blair Jackson, Reid recounted how he assembled his comedy material on the trip from New York:

> *Peter Sellers was on the flight down to Washington, accompanied by two PR men; and Benny Goodman also, accompanied by a couple of pals. I was accompanied only by The New York Times, but that was all I needed. There on the front page was, obviously, my first question in this "press conference": The indictment of U.S. Steel on the previous day! ... (Only one person) heard this until I walked out and did it for the elite of this world: political dignitaries and journalists! You've got to admit it—this was one hell of a place to break in untried material!*

Before JFK and a few thousand guests, Reid played both the questioner and the President...

> Q: *Sir, I would like to ask one more question about steel. The companies had a rather difficult time yesterday, and I'm wondering whether in view of this, and of course the other events, if you still feel that the Administration will be able to have a congenial relationship with these companies?*

> JFK: *I hope that we will. (Audience reacts to the distinctive voice.) This is not an easy matter. (Longer hoots and hollers.) I'm very hopeful that we can have an extremely friendly and cordial relation. In fact, that's what we have. ...*
> (In attendance was visiting British Prime Minister Harold Macmillan.)
> JFK: *Great Britain is our oldest and best ally. It's possible she's our only ally. ...*
> (Regarding automated subways in New York City)
> JFK: *Let us never automate out of fear, but let us never fear to automate.*

In an interview with the author Studs Terkel, Reid provided context: "I think this was, perhaps, the first impression of President Kennedy, certainly that he had ever heard or any of these other correspondents heard." A staunch supporter of progressive politics, Reid said he was "extremely sympathetic and friendly to the president, even though I picked out little oddities of speech and so on, which we're all familiar with." *Time* magazine wrote that "Kennedy was convulsed" as he watched Reid's performance.

After the show, the president invited Reid to appear with him at a Democratic fundraiser the following month at New York's Madison Square Garden. That spectacle lives on in history—though not because of Reid's contribution. This was the night that Marilyn Monroe, clad in a sequined gown so tight it seemed painted upon her curves, cooed "Happy birthday, Mister President." JFK, seated in an upholstered chair with his feet up

**At the White House Correspondents' Dinner in 1962, from left:
Elliott Reid, John Kennedy, Peter Sellers, Harold Macmillan.**

and smoking a cigar, seemed captivated by every minute of his 45th birthday bash, with entertainment provided by Monroe, Harry Belafonte, Peter Lawford, Peggy Lee, Henry Fonda, Maria Callas, Ella Fitzgerald and Jack Benny ("The amazing thing to me is how a man in a rocking chair can have such a young wife"). And, doing a four-minute presidential impersonation, Elliott Reid.

(From the Small World Department: Reid played Ernie Malone opposite Monroe in the 1953 film "Gentlemen Prefer Blondes," in which she famously sang "Diamonds Are a Girl's Best Friend.")

Reid's routine at the Garden, little noted nor long remembered, was a benchmark occurrence: The conflation of comedy and politics in a form that until 1962 was virtually unheard of. The following night he took his act a few blocks uptown and performed it for a national TV audience on "The Ed Sullivan Show." Though Kennedy himself praised Reid's work, it didn't make much of an impression on viewers or media observers. Perhaps Reid's sophisticated takes on serious political topics were difficult for a mainstream audience to appreciate, despite his slick mimicry of JFK's voice and mannerisms. Much like the Peter Principle in business, Reid's insider act kept being promoted— from a savvy D.C. audience, to a polished crowd of Democratic high rollers, and finally to folks watching Ed Sullivan's program

Following the Madison Square Garden event, Elliott Reid did his JFK for guests at a private party hosted by presidential advisor Arthur Krim.

—until it reached its highest level of ineffectiveness. Regardless, Elliott Reid, who died in 2013, was a true pioneer in comedy and politics.

He once explained, "I'm not interested in saying, 'My next impression is' or 'and then who showed up at the Hollywood party' and you do Edward G. Robinson. That kind of mimicry is still being done, but it's regrettable I think." He stressed that he was not trying "to impose any great message of my own, but I think it's implicit in what I do."

Meanwhile, in France, a comic impersonator by the name of Henri Tisot created quite a stir with a record album in which he mimicked President De Gaulle. Remarkably, the disc sold over 1 million copies.

As for JFK and those who would poke fun his way, columnist Russell Baker wrote in *The New York Times* that "one of the Kennedy Administration's brighter achievements in 1962 has been its restoration of the sound of laughter."

By year's end, the laughs would become record-breaking.

2 / Follow-the-Meader

In the summer of 1962, the Kennedy Administration faced a sliding stock market, a crisis in steel production and a setback in Congress on important farm legislation. Yet, as Tom Wicker reported in *The New York Times* on July 3, John F. Kennedy's popularity remained high—in fact, it was growing.

That night, the charismatic young president's appeal was tested in an unexpected way during the CBS broadcast of "Talent Scouts," a showcase for up-and-coming performers. Each newcomer was introduced by a celebrity, and for this installment the guests were singer Robert Goulet, actor Van Johnson, singer-actress Sheree North, boxer Floyd Patterson and the rising star Carol Burnett. Host Jim Backus presented the night's most intriguing act: "I know you're going to be delighted with the TV debut of Mr. Vaughn Meader."

To robust applause—cued by a flashing sign pointed at the studio audience that said PLEASE APPLAUD—the slender 26-year-old, with dark hair, black suit and thin black tie, began his 8-minute act. "Thank you. There must be some mistake. I'm not really a comedian; you see, I'm a collector. And right now I'm busy collecting—well, famous political quotations is what I'm working on now. For instance, I'm sure you all know the famous one from Sen. Bill Forgets of Arizona, who was quoted as saying: 'My immigration bill would permit more foreign neighbors to visit our shores and at the same time keep out the alien element.'"

After a few more mildly amusing fake quotes, Meader segued to a bit about the world in 2022 via "a newscast 60 years from now." Example: "Macon, Georgia, July 3, 2022. Bus terminals in Macon were peacefully integrated today. Attorney General Rogers hailed this progress and stated that plans for gradual school integration would soon follow." The studio audience, while polite, was clearly losing interest in Meader's political quips—tepid versions of material popularized at the time by comedy mavericks such as Mort Sahl and Lenny Bruce. Meader closed his "newscast" by wishing "a happy 67th birthday to President Caroline Kennedy."

Halfway into his act, Meader said, "You're probably wondering by now why I talk so much about politics. Well, a certain politician has had a great effect on my life. Let me show you what I mean." He walked to a small lectern and, imitating the distinctive Boston accent and hand gestures that Americans had come to know so well during JFK's Camelot, explained...

"You see, I used to be a top nightclub comedian. For the past three years there's someone going around this country imitating me!"

The audience murmured slightly as Meader began. After his first full sentence, a woman shrieked. Laughter and applause built, seemingly because of the sight and sound of Meader's portrayal more so than anything he said. He conducted a mock press

Kennedy and Meader meet the media.

conference, with confederates posing questions...

> Q: *Sir, could you comment on the African situation please?*
> A: *Well, I'm not up to date on that. Now, I sent a personal representative to Africa some months ago, and so far she hasn't even dropped me a card.*

At this point the audience was laughing heartily, especially when hearing the word c-ahh-d with the thickest Boston cadence.

> Q: *When did you become concerned about economics?*
> A: *Well, I, uh, became concerned about economics during the depression, a couple of Mondays ago.*
> Q: *When are we going to send a man to the moon?*
> A: *Whenever Mr. Goldwater wants to go.*

A "reporter" then asked if the president had any final comments. Meader stepped forward to say, "Yes, I'd like to make one final statement at this time." Changing from Kennedy's voice to his own he continued, "And I would like to make that final statement as myself, Vaughn Meader. And that is to say thank you to the United States, a country where it is possible for a young comedian like myself to come out on television before millions of people and kid its leading citizen. Thank you. Good night."

Meader's disclaimer was even more remarkable than the JFK impersonation itself. Imagine the likes of Dana Carvey or Alec Baldwin back-peddling that way after skewering the president. But in the early sixties such performances didn't exist—at least not on prime-time network television—except for the appearance by Elliott Reid that managed to sneak under the radar a few months earlier.

Fearing that his on-air explanation wouldn't suffice, Meader sent a letter to Washington:

> Dear Mister President:
>
> I respectfully call your attention to the Talent Scout Show which we taped last night for viewing on CBS Television Tuesday night, July 3, 10:00 PM.
>
> I impersonated you but I did it with great affection and respect. Hope it meets with your approval.
>
>> Respectfully,
> > Vaughn Meader

Reflecting on the broadcast, Carol Burnett told me: "We didn't have much contact with the performers. I do recall Meader being very nice."

Not long after appearing on "Talent Scouts," Burnett found herself in the Oval Office, meeting with JFK. Along with Judy Garland and Danny Kaye, she was planning an entertainment event for the president. "The matter of Vaughn Meader's impression was mentioned," she remembers. "Kennedy responded, 'He sounds more like Teddy!'"

◆ ◆ ◆

ABBOTT VAUGHN MEADER was born in 1936 in Waterville, Maine—where the word "water" would have an eerie relevance in his youth. His grandfather died going over a waterfall in a barrel, and Meader's father drowned while swimming, a year after his only child was born. His mother, a heavy drinker, worked miles away in Boston as a cocktail waitress, so Abbott lived with various relatives, attending five high schools before he graduated. In 1953 he joined the Army and was stationed at Mannheim, West Germany, where he worked as a lab technician and also played in a band called The Rhine Rangers. Discharged four years later, he returned to Maine with his German bride, Vera, and sold sewing machines door-to-door before moving to New York to study broadcasting.

Dropping his first name, Vaughn Meader began doing an act at the Blue Angel club in Greenwich Village. While ad-libbing about the Kennedys one night, he tossed in a quick impersonation of the president, which the patrons loved. Gradually he expanded the routine, taking questions from the audience.

◆ ◆ ◆

WHILE PRESIDENTIAL PARODIES were emerging in club acts, two young media entrepreneurs, Bob Booker and Earle Doud, were creating an album-length spoof that would target JFK and his entire family.

From his home in Northern California, as he neared his 91st birthday in 2022, Booker recounted for me how things unfolded 60 years earlier...

"Starving to death in New York City, we were looking for the next big thing. It was a good time for the country, the promise for the future was beyond belief.

"Comedy albums, the kind done by Shelley Berman and Bob Newhart, were popular. But John Kennedy was the biggest star in the world. Here was a young man with a beautiful wife. He was funny, he was amusing, he was great. We figured why not do an album about him? Earle and I finished the script for 'The First Family,' but we needed someone to play Kennedy."

When Vaughn Meader made his appearance on "Talent Scouts," Booker and Doud took note, as did many newspapers, including *The Boston Globe*, which called his JFK routine "the brightest item of the night." Yet, the concept was so untested, it prompted some critics, like Win Fanning of the *Pittsburgh Post-Gazette*, to write: "I'm not strong for imitations of any kind, especially of the President. However, as Meader handled his mimicry with both good humor and good taste, I'll reluctantly make an exception in this case."

Booker and Doud invited several actors to audition for their "The First Family" album, but awarding Meader the JFK role was never really in question. His stock was soaring across the showbiz spectrum, culminating on October 7 in the best gig of all: a spot on "The Ed Sullivan Show." With the Cuban missile crisis dominating the news, Meader updated his "press conference" bit...

Q: *You recently sent an agent into Cuba. Did he return with any information?*
A: *Well, I didn't send him for information, I sent him for cigars.*

But even with widespread acceptance of his act, Meader felt compelled to close with another dose of rationalization to viewers: "I'm sure you realize, especially keeping in mind the news of the last couple of weeks, it's a lot easier to impersonate a president than it is to be one. "

Following Meader's "Ed Sullivan" appearance he joined Booker's troupe to record a 30-minute acetate demo of "The First Family" material. At the time Booker was filling in for the renowned DJ Murray the K (Kaufman) on WINS radio, so he had easy access to record companies. But after listening to Booker's demo a dozen execs said no, among them Leonard Goldenson, president of ABC. Present in that meeting was James Hagerty, former press secretary to President Eisenhower and now part of ABC's brass. He pronounced "The First Family" routines "degrading to the presidency," adding "every communist country in the world would love this record."

After Hagerty left the room Goldenson remarked, "He doesn't know what the fuck he's talking about." According to Booker, "Leonard smiled at us and said, 'It's a giant hit. I can't touch it but I'll tell you who to take it to, because he's a one man show; doesn't have my problems.' And he called Archie Bleyer and set a meeting for us the next morning."

Bleyer ran the smaller Cadence Records, which had hits with the Everly Brothers and Andy Williams, but lost both to bigger labels when their contracts expired. "Archie loved it," says Booker. "He gave us the money we needed to set up a recording date."

♦ ♦ ♦

ON THE NIGHT OF OCTOBER 22, President Kennedy announced a naval blockade of Cuba, based on surveillance showing the Soviets had installed as many as 40 nuclear missiles on the island. "The cost of freedom is always high," he told a worried nation, "but Americans have always paid it."

As Kennedy spoke, Bob Booker and Earle Doud gathered their performers at a Manhattan studio on West 57th Street to record "The First Family" before an invited audience of about 150 people. Concerned that the news from Washington would inhibit the production, Booker had television sets in the studio disconnected so no one could hear the real-life president's dire words. "Archie was in the booth about to faint," recalls Booker, "because he had heard the news about Cuba."

Meader took the stage, along with Naomi Brossart in the role of Jackie Kennedy...

JACKIE: *Family, family, family. Jack, there's just too much family. Can't we ever get away alone?*
JFK: *Jackie, I promise we'll get away tomorrow. No more, uh, family for a while. I promise. Now, uhh, turn off the light. Good night, Jackie.*
JACKIE: *Good night, Jack.*
JFK: *Good night, Bobby. Good night, Ethel.*
OTHERS: *Good night, Jack. Good night, Teddy. Good night, Eunice.*

When the album was released 22 days later, Booker managed to have it played on WINS radio for three straight hours. The result was the fastest-selling pre-Beatles record, with over 7.5 million copies sold, and to this day history's most successful comedy album. "The First Family" won the Grammy for Album of the Year and Meader received one for Best Comedy Performance. He was profiled in *Life* and *Time* magazines and appeared on numerous TV shows including "What's My Line?"—where he used a half-dozen voices trying to fool the blind-folded panel, but was nevertheless identified rather quickly.

If there is such a thing as overnight success, Meader was that. According to the story in *Life*, he went from earning $7.50 a night at the Blue Angel, to commanding $5,000 for a New Years Eve gig. He also opened the door for more presidential parodies. Just two weeks after his turn on "Talent Scouts" the show presented another unknown comedian named George Carlin, and he, too, mimicked JFK. What seemed to be an instant transformation of America's willingness to accept an imitation of a sitting president had taken 173 years.

The Kennedy Administration provided a perfect storm. At 43 Kennedy was the youngest person ever elected president. He had leading-man good looks, a quick wit, a stunning wife and charming kids. "The First Family" exploited all this in a positive way, almost like the popular sitcoms "Ozzie and Harriet" and "Father Knows Best," in which the male lead was the occasional brunt of mild jokes, but in the end was revered. In years to follow, presidents would be portrayed harshly, but Vaughn Meader's act was a valentine to JFK...

> ...JFK divides up the bath toys: *Nine of the PT boats, two of the Yogi Bear beach balls, the ball of silly putty belong to Caroline. Nine of the PT boats, one of the Yogi Bear beach balls, and the two Howdy Doody plastic bouncing clowns are baby John's. The rub-bah swan is mine.*
>
> ...Jackie conducts a White House tour: *This is the Blue Room. We decided to leave it just the way President Blue had it originally.*
>
> ...JFK answers the front door: *(Boy) Can Caroline come out and play? (JFK) I'm sorry, young man, but she can't. She's in Italy with her mother. (Boy) Well, then, what's Lyndon doing?*

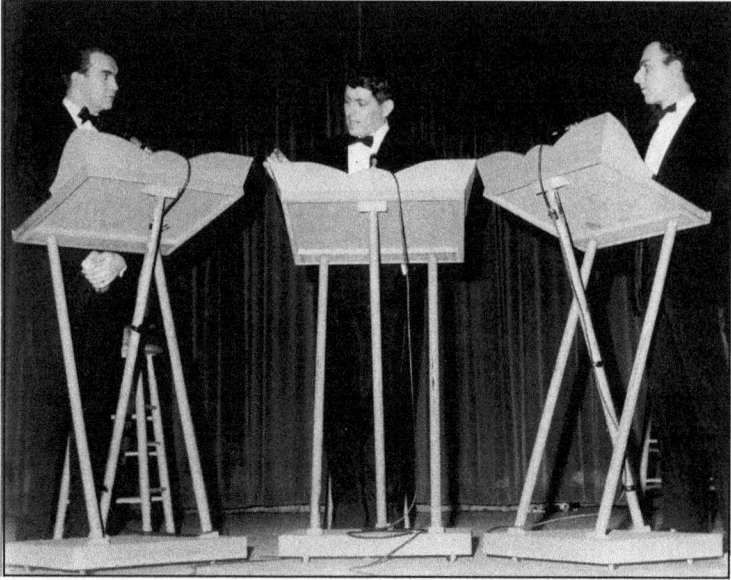

On stage at Carnegie Hall, Vaughn Meader, center, is joined by supporting players for routines from "The First Family."

Meader's New England roots certainly helped him with the thick Boston accent, but his Kennedy impersonation went beyond that—the vocal tone was almost perfect. According to historian Nicholas Cull of the Annenberg School at the University of Southern California, shortly after the album was released, presidential advisor Arthur Schlesinger was driving to the White House and believed he was listening to a radio broadcast of a live news conference...

> REPORTER: *Now that you are in office, what do you think the chances are of a Jewish president?*
> JFK: *Well, I think they're pretty good. Let me say, I don't see why a person of the Jewish faith can't be president of the United States. I know that as a Catholic I could never vote for him, but other than that...*

After learning it was a spoof, Schlesinger wrote a memo to the president in which he declared, "This raises the question of what in hell a president of the United States ought to do about mimicry." The short answer to Schlesinger's query was "nothing," as JFK made a point of praising the album—at least in public. According to Bob Booker, "Kennedy bought 100 copies and gave them out as gifts. I said why didn't you just ask? I would have given him the albums for free."

The historical record is murky about JFK's true feelings. At a dinner with the Democratic National Committee, the president began his remarks: "Vaughn Meader was busy tonight, so I came myself." But in private Kennedy expressed some frustration about the album's popularity. Jackie Kennedy was more aggressive, criticizing the portrayal of Caroline and John Jr., which she felt should have been off limits. In private papers revealed in 1969, Mrs. Kennedy wrote to an aide: "I don't care what [Meader] says about us, but the fact that he dares mention my children's names to make himself an extra dollar, I don't

Meader meets fans at a store in New York City.

like that. I would just like him to know that I consider him a rat as far as the children are concerned." Mrs. Kennedy reportedly pressured her husband to have the FCC block radio stations from playing "The First Family," but the nation was in love with the album, just as it was with its president.

♦ ♦ ♦

WITH THE SUCCESS OF THEIR ALBUM, Booker and Doud took the cast on the road for live, on-stage presentations of the album's content. The first show, at Carnegie Hall, was standing room only, despite a newspaper strike and a raging snowstorm. The producers also went to work on Volume Two, but Meader, who was making big money on TV as well as with live appearances, balked. He was growing tired of the Kennedy routine and hated being pigeon-holed in the role. "He told me he wanted to go back to doing his act," says Booker. "I told him, 'Sorry. You don't have an act. You're good at playing this character.' Vaughn just wasn't a very funny person."

Booker hired a man to travel with Meader and make sure he stuck to the material. He also filed a lawsuit demanding that Meader participate in the second album, which went forward and was released in Spring of 1963. The new album was more slickly produced and was arguably funnier than the first, because it mocked not only the Kennedys but the original recording as well. Volume Two begins with JFK taking his popular press conferences to prime time, where the events are dressed up with song and dance in the style of a Broadway musical.

In another bit, Jack calls a meeting with brothers Ted and Bobby to discuss an important family matter. "I'm the older brother," says Jack, "and I had this voice first. I do believe that you two should find your own voices, just like I did." Meader plays all three parts, demonstrating considerable skill in portraying subtle differences among the brothers who did, after all, sound very much alike. Jack suggests they might adjust their intonation of certain words. The word "vig-ah," for example, might be pronounced by Bobby as "vig-gure."

Meanwhile, the floodgates opened on presidential parodies, with copycats referred to by *Billboard Magazine* as "Follow-the-Meader albums." One, by William Hirsch, who did a spot-on JFK impression, was unabashedly titled, "The Family in the White House." Comedian Chuck McCann, who played bit parts in "The First Family," released a musical collection called "Sing Along with Jack."

Larry Foster rushed out a song parody called "My Christmas Message to the World," in which he imitated JFK in a sappy little number written by the comedian Marty Brill. A few months later the two teamed to create the album "The Other Family," spoofing Soviet Premier Nikita Khrushchev. It begins with a phone call from Moscow to the White House...

Krushchev: *Hello, hello? Little girl, let me speak to poppa. (pause) Never mind who this is little girl. I want talk to your poppa. (pause) I don't care if he's on his rocker or off his rocker, I still want to talk with your poppa. (pause) All right, this is Premier...uh, this is Uncle Nick. (pause) No, not the one with the bag and the reindeer, that's Saint Nick!*

There was even an album in Spanish called "The Last Family," in which Tito Hernandez plays Cuba's Fidel Castro, residing in the Red House rather than the White House.

◆ ◆ ◆

ONE YEAR AFTER "The First Family" was released—53 weeks, to be precise—Vaughn Meader was getting into a taxi at the airport in Milwaukee when the driver asked, "Did you hear about Kennedy in Dallas?" Thinking it was the formulaic set-up to a joke, Meader replied, "No. How does it go?"

Informed that the president had been shot, Meader found the nearest bar, got drunk, and then took the next flight home. Although he would live for another 41 years (succumbing in 2004 to pulmonary disease), more than one observer has noted that part of Meader, his career, died that day.

At about the same moment on November 22, Bob Booker was having lunch in Greenwich Village with the writer-poet Allen Ginsberg. "Allen always brought along someone interesting at our lunches—someone who wanted a free meal—and that day it was Bob Dylan." The meal was interrupted by a call from Booker's secretary, relaying the news from Dallas. The three men sat stunned.

Booker and Archie Bleyer immediately contacted record distributors and insisted that all copies of both "First Family" albums be recalled and destroyed. "I wasn't going to make money off the death of Jack Kennedy," Booker says emphatically.

Lenny Bruce went on stage at a Greenwich Village club, and his first words to the patrons summed it up: "Boy, Vaughn Meader is fucked."

Meader abandoned his JFK material, but did create other comedy albums. One was a hodgepodge of political bits titled "Have Some Nuts!!!" In 1971 he moved beyond playing the president with an album called "The Second Coming," in which he portrayed Jesus Christ. "Playing the president was easy," he told the *Los Angeles Times,* "but playing God was a bitch." Both albums flopped. Meader's personal life—he was married four times—his health and his career all suffered. He went back to the name Abbott Meader, and performed in Maine with a country music group. A few years before his death, he was interviewed by CBS News, and toward the end was asked to do "the voice" one last time. Whether Meader had anticipated the request, or simply ad-libbed a response, he used his haunting JFK voice to say this:

"Two hundred years ago in Concord, Massachusetts a shot was fired that was heard around the world. Thirty-seven years ago in Dallas, Texas another shot was fired that was heard around the world. The first bullet fired from the Concord bridge signaled the birth of the American spirit. The second bullet fired from the Texas book depository attempted to end that spirit and we've seen in the last thirty something years how nearly successful that second bullet was. But in the final analysis there is no bullet, there is no bomb, there is no power on the face of this Earth that can destroy the American spirit. "

Abbott Meader had no apparent bitterness. He made his exit exhibiting the same positivity he brought to "The First Family" album, whose liner notes include: "No one has more respect for the high offices and the people suggested here than do those of us who had a hand in putting this together."

After Kennedy's death, Bob Booker received offers to do an album about the new president. He declined. "I told them there's nothing funny about Lyndon Johnson."

That's a matter of comedic and political opinion.

Regardless, it didn't stop others from portraying the sitting president—a gimmick that had never been done in any significant way until Booker and Meader came along, but something that would soon become a staple in American politics.

3 / *With a heavy heart*

Those old enough to remember hearing the news from Dallas on November 22, 1963, know how it feels when an entire nation goes numb. The president was dead, Camelot was finished, the laughter had stopped.

Lyndon Johnson shared most of John Kennedy's political views, though after assuming the presidency Johnson was even more committed to civil rights and broad government assistance programs that came to be known as the Great Society. But by every measure that made the youthful JFK admired—and the perfect object of gentle parody in "The First Family"—LBJ was the opposite: a lumbering 6-foot-4 career politician with uncool eyeglasses and a Texas drawl. Kennedy had leading-man good looks, while Johnson's weathered face seemed to be made from mismatched parts.

The months following the assassination proved to be somewhat of a grace period for LBJ. Comedians and impressionists who had sharpened their skills with the Kennedy family backed off—at least temporarily. "People wanted to laugh," observed Sheldon Patinkin of the Second City troupe, "but I don't think anyone knew what to laugh at, or if they could."

The comedic ceasefire finally ended with an import from British television called "That Was the Week That Was" (commonly, "TW3"). Produced for the BBC and hosted by 23-year-old David Frost, the series was a forerunner of edgy news-driven comedy like that on John Oliver's "Last Week Tonight," and SNL's "Weekend Update." "TW3" creator Ned Sherrin described his show in a BBC memo: "Aware, pointed, irreverent, fundamentally serious, intelligently witty, outspoken in the proper sense of the word." Though designed for a British audience, it dwelled heavily on news from America, with material that was jarring—even by today's standards on cable channels and streaming services. How jarring? In one sketch, the show's lead vocalist Millicent Martin—later a Tony winner on Broadway—dressed as a sexy Uncle Sam and was joined by a male chorus in black face to sing about the American South...

> I want to go back to Mississippi,
> Where the scent of blossoms kiss the evening breeze;
> Where the Mississippi mud,
> Kind of mingles with the blood,
> Of the niggers who are hanging from the branches in the trees.

Over 10 million people watched "TW3" each week, making instant celebrities of cast members like William Rushton, who imitated and mocked Prime Minister Harold Macmillan. The show also featured actors in the roles of American politicians, which British viewers seemed to enjoy as much as parodies of their own leaders. Based on the success of the BBC show, NBC purchased rights to an American version, a preview

"TW3" with Elliott Reid, Henry Morgan, host David Frost
and singer Nancy Ames, in 1964.

of which was broadcast in the fall of 1963, with Henry Fonda as host. "By network standards the show marked a new and welcome freedom in irreverent comment," said critic Jack Gould in *The New York Times*, although he found "the humor was only intermittent." Twelve days later Kennedy was assassinated and further installments of NBC's series were delayed. Meanwhile, the British version was canceled despite record high ratings, under pressure from the governing Tories who claimed topical comedy would interfere with England's coming general election. David Frost called the cancellation "a great compliment" but wondered whether an election year was not "when it's needed most." Frost reasoned, "People are tired of hearing a lot of morale-boosting nonsense. They want to hear the truth."

"TW3" joined NBC's weekly schedule on January 10, 1964, with Frost as host and an American cast that included Buck Henry, Alan Alda, Henry Morgan and Elliott Reid. Born out of British comedic sensibility, the series rode a wave of change that was sweeping America. Everything that was buttoned-down and proper during the Kennedy years seemed to explode during Johnson's presidency—from crazy clothes to psychedelic drugs; from civil rights marches to Vietnam war protests.

Johnson's efforts to sell Americans on the rapidly expanding war were mocked by "TW3," as an actor playing LBJ sang...

When they asked about my policy
On the fighting in Vietnam
I made 'em laugh
I made 'em laugh!
They said about that war the folks
At home don't really give a damn
Well, I made 'em laugh
I made 'em laugh!
I said, "I've got a fabulous idea that really is uncanny
Let's make the war more popular with junior and with granny
Let's call it what it really is
A shootin' hootenanny!
Oh, boy
Well, I made 'em laugh!

Vaughn Meader's Kennedy routines had opened the door to mocking sitting presidents, but the tough stuff dished by "TW3" was unprecedented. Meader and his producers had been among Kennedy's biggest fans; their sketches were unabashedly pro-JFK and they took pains to stress that their jokes were rooted in love and admiration. Johnson would be treated differently, with a focus on policy as well as personality. But the "TW3" efforts notwithstanding, a comedic barrage against LBJ was slow in starting, especially because his Republican opponent in 1964 was the eminently mockable Arizona Senator Barry Goldwater. Goldwater was seen as a dangerous extremist who spoke, at least semi-seriously, about using nuclear weapons in Vietnam. "TW3" took aim at Goldwater regularly, but in the period leading up to Election Day Republicans concocted a clever scheme to keep "TW3" off the air: The GOP purchased program-length commercial blocks in the "TW3" time slot, forcing its preemption for three weeks. (A fourth preemption was caused by network coverage of the death of former President Herbert Hoover). The preemptions blunted the impact "TW3" had on Goldwater's campaign, but it hardly mattered. Johnson won in a landslide with 61 percent of the vote.

♦ ♦ ♦

HISTORIAN DORIS KEARNS GOODWIN, who worked with Johnson and authored his biography, offers a description of the man that is a virtual template for impressionists: "Terrified of making slips swearing or using ungrammatical constructions," she writes, "Johnson insisted on reading from formal texts. Facial muscles frozen in place, except for the simpering smile, he projected an image of feigned propriety, dullness, and dishonesty."

Cue David Frye.

Like other comedians of the period, Frye—born David Shapiro—developed his act in Greenwich Village nightclubs. Short and stocky, with pudgy cheeks and a somewhat oversized nose, Frye was more than an impressionist. He was the rare performer who could contort his face so that, without the wigs and facial appliances used nowadays on "Saturday Night Live," he managed to deliver a visual as well as vocal impression. One of Frye's contemporaries, Robert Klein, marveled, "He actually seemed to become, body and soul, the person he was imitating."

Frye's LBJ had a drooping hound-dog face and elevated eyebrows, plus the exact simpering smile that Goodwin described. With a syrupy southern drawl he'd declare: "Ah come here as uh simple barefoot boy from Texas who has become yore king."

"I first found this talent in myself in my teens," Frye told *Esquire* in 1971. "I would meet some person, it could be anybody, on the street, in a store, who had this attraction about him. Later on I would begin to believe I was that person. I would make his facial expressions, imitate his voice. ... Maybe this is some kind of psychic phenomenon, to feel as if you are somebody else."

With Johnson elected to a full term, Frye got his big break on "The Ed Sullivan Show." As with Vaughn Meader, the audience seemed captivated by a performer who sounded and even looked like the president, while the jokes themselves were almost beside the point...

> *Ah come here tonight with a heavy heart* (audience responds with significant laughter).
> *We must do something to end the problems in this great land of ours* (moderate laughs).
> *So I have decided to take the following step...* (Frye takes one giant step forward on the stage and the audience erupts with laughter and applause).

This was the nature of most presidential parodies during the sixties, performed by skilled impressionists, many of whom didn't seem interested in influencing public opinion. "TW3" was a notable exception, but the NBC series was canceled after just 15 months.

◆ ◆ ◆

AT AGE 23, ALAN MYERSON was a director at Chicago's Second City, where presidential impersonations evolved—with Andrew Duncan doing John Kennedy bits even before Vaughn Meader came along. In 1962 Myerson married a member of the troupe, Irene Riordan, and the couple set off on a cross-country drive that included a San Francisco honeymoon. With $60,000 raised from friends, they launched an improvisational group called The Committee, named after the reviled House Un-American Activities Committee (created in the late thirties to investigate allegedly subversive behavior on the part of private citizens). "We're all in the same boat and it's sinking," said Myerson as he set up his theater at 622 Broadway, in what had been an

Actress Barbara Bosson, later of "Hill Street Blues," at the theater.

Italian restaurant with an indoor bocce-ball court. "We're all accomplices in a hypocritical world. Our job is to walk through it, pointing."

In decades following The Committee's closing in 1974, Myerson worked primarily as a television director, with credits that included "The Bob Newhart Show" and "The Garry Shandling Show." When I first interviewed him in 2021, Donald Trump had been defeated and the Biden Administration was being formed. At age 84 Myerson hadn't lost his concern about hypocrisy; in fact, I got the feeling he was more concerned about it than ever.

"Second City took a gentle, liberal approach," he said about the Chicago troupe that many considered quite daring in the early sixties. "The Committee was more left wing, much more interested in making commentary. We were very active politically." Myerson's proudest moment occurred in early '68, following the State of the Union speech by President Johnson. "The enemy has been defeated in battle after battle," Johnson had bellowed about a war that killed more than 57,000 American military personnel and countless Vietnamese civilians. He added, "Our goal is peace—and peace at the earliest possible moment."

Watching the speech in a Bay Area living room were three members of The Committee troupe: Howard Hesseman (later Dr. Johnny Fever on "WKRP"), Garry Goodrow (actor and jazz musician) and Mimi Fariña (Joan Baez's sister). The group grew agitated over Johnson's defense of the unpopular war, but Hesseman completely lost it when the president turned to a domestic matter: "This year, I will propose a Drug Control Act to provide stricter penalties for those who traffic in LSD and other

Chris Ross as LBJ, performing with The Committee.

dangerous drugs with our people." As Myerson tells it, "We were in San Francisco! LSD was no stranger to us, and we were no stranger to it."

The next night Myerson proposed an improvisational scenario recreating the viewing experience. Actor Chris Ross had done some LBJ impressions for the group, but this time Peter Bonerz ("The Bob Newhart Show" and "Murphy Brown") played the part, wearing a cowboy hat and gesturing like Johnson, while stage manager Jim Cranna read from an actual transcript of the speech.

On stage:

Hesseman is angry and tries to turn off the TV...the others stop him...but his fury builds and finally he mimes turning off the TV...but it won't go off! Bonerz continues to gesticulate as Cranna's voice booms, "You can't turn me off, I'm you!...You can't turn me off, I'm you," as a mantra for the 40 minute length of the piece. Hesseman breaks the fourth wall and tells the audience about the anger he experienced the night before..."I'm a nonviolent hippie"...yet..."it felt good to hate this motherfucker." He encourages the crowd to channel its own hate against Johnson, as all eight cast members pick up the chant: "It's fun to hate!"... and now the audience is shouting back, "Stop! Don't make me do this!"

As the patrons' frenzy approaches a dangerous level, Myerson gives a signal from the back of the house to turn it off—in fact, to turn it around. "For a while that felt good," Hesseman tells the audience, "but I don't think we can kill this guy with our hatred. Maybe we can kill him with love." Cast members begin to demonstrate love for each other...the audience follows the lead, singing and dancing in the aisles. After several minutes, the stage suddenly goes black. In darkness, Mimi sings out, "Vietnam!" (And scene.)

"Howard had turned the audience on a dime," recalls Myerson, "in an ecstatic, almost evangelical way. It was a real love-in. After piece, titled 'The Exorcism,' the audience wouldn't leave.

"In my universe of experiences as an improvising director, it was the most successful single moment for me. We got calls about it for weeks, but we never did it again."

◆ ◆ ◆

NOT EVERYONE who could do a good LBJ saw the need to grind a political ax...

"I never wanted to upset anybody or put anybody down or talk about any particular group of people, I just went along, and I made people laugh. I wasn't trying to hurt anybody."

The speaker is John Byner, one of the most acclaimed impressionists in the sixties and for decades to follow—a man who none other than Bob Booker, creator of "The First Family" album, says is the best he's ever heard. I reached Byner at his home in Florida, and his autobiographical remarks included much of what we've heard from his contemporaries: A childhood filled with impressing friends and family with his uncanny ability to imitate voices...an act that developed in a small club on Long Island, and then on stages in Greenwich Village...a break on the CBS program "Talent Scouts," followed by a shot on "The Ed Sullivan Show"...in all, what he summarizes as "A lifetime of laughter."

Byner was 22 when Kennedy took office, creating "a goldmine for impressionists." In one bit he imagined JFK as a college football coach with a thick Boston accent, giving a pep talk at halftime...

Men, I realize the situation doesn't look good and want you to know that when I agreed to play against these Texas Longhorns, I had no idea that we'd be playing against real steers! Which brings us to today. When we lose today, and...we...uh...WILL...lose... today...

After Vaughn Meader's "First Family" album dropped, Byner drove into Manhattan from Baldwin, Long Island and paid a dollar to enter a JFK Impression Contest. "A lot of agents came to see what was going on, and Meader himself was in the audience. I won first prize—ten dollars. As I was leaving Meader stopped me and said, 'Hey, you're pretty good. And I don't say that to everybody.'"

Did you know Meader after that?

"I got to know him a little bit, yeah. Unfortunately, later on in the '70s I was in LA, walking down the street, and here comes a guy with a shopping cart. Nothing in it, just pushing the shopping cart, and it was Vaughn Meader. And he was trying to make a buck playing piano and singing then. He had nicotine stains all over his fingers from smoking so hard. His hair had grown. He didn't look so good."

By the late sixties Byner was making regular appearances on variety shows and talk programs (his Ed Sullivan impression, done as a recurring bit on Sullivan's show, was one of the best) but he stayed away from politics. Then, booked as a guest on the hit sitcom "Get Smart," he arrived for rehearsal and was handed a script indicating: John does the voice of Lyndon Johnson.

Had you ever done Johnson?

"No. I had never even thought of doing him."

So what did you do?

"You know, I have like a mind's ear. And if I can hear my mind, like 'do John Wayne,' I just replicate it from my mind. I can hear it in my mind. And I do it. That's how it works."

In the scene, dastardly foreign spies at KAOS phone Maxwell Smart (Don Adams) and his boss, Thaddeus, at CONTROL, convincing them they are speaking with President Johnson (Byner), who summarily names the bumbling Max as the agency's new chief. The Johnson impression is spot-on, but the jokes are tepid. Byner never did LBJ again, insisting, "I'm just not very political."

◆ ◆ ◆

FOLLOWING THE PHENOMENAL SUCCESS of "The First Family," record companies were looking for similar parodies about LBJ. Bob Booker would have no part of it, but his partner in the Kennedy project, Earle Doud, set out to find a different way to mock a sitting president. The resulting album, "Welcome to the LBJ Ranch!" on Capitol Records, used Johnson's actual voice, plus voices of other prominent politicians. The audio clips, taken from news conferences and other public events, were spliced together with fake questions delivered by actors to create humorous "dialogue"...

> REPORTER: *Mr. President, as a continuing example of your policies, who in the years to come will be guarding our eastern coast against Russian submarines?*
> LBJ: *Thirty Cuban fishermen.*
> REPORTER: *Mr. President. We understand that you are contemplating some changes in the income tax law for next year.*
> LBJ: *That's what we propose to do.*
> REPORTER: *And if your changes go through sir, how much of our net salary will we be able to keep?*
> LBJ: *One-tenth of one percent.*

This technique of mixing audio from different sources was popular on comedy albums in the sixties. Radio DJs found the material to be a welcome change of pace. Today, the humor seems so thin it would hardly provoke a chuckle, yet the studio audience at the taping of the "LBJ Ranch" howled with laughter at almost every word. Earle Doud, who died in 1998, claimed that his album was played by 90 percent of U.S. radio stations.

"Fortunately," he wrote in liner notes, "we still live in a society which accepts free expression and appreciates a healthy, honest laugh." Indeed, he managed to produce a follow-up titled "Lyndon Johnson's Lonely Hearts Club Band"—released in 1967, shortly after the Beatles' "Sergeant Pepper" album. But the tide of public opinion was running against Doud's meek approach and against Johnson's policies. A more biting style of humor was taking hold.

◆ ◆ ◆

BARBARA GARSON'S STAGE PLAY "MACBIRD!" shocked audiences when it opened at New York's Village Gate Theater on February 27, 1967. Starring Stacy Keach as Lyndon Johnson, the brutal satire superimposed the Kennedy assassination onto the plot of Shakespeare's "Macbeth," with JFK becoming "John Ken

The program from the Village Gate Theater in March, 1967, with Stacy Keach as MacBird and Rue McClanahan as Lady MacBird.

O'Dunc," and LBJ "MacBird." The play wove together sequences from Shakespearean tragedies including "Macbeth," "Hamlet," and "Richard III."

Garson, an anti-war activist living in Berkeley, California, insisted her play was not seriously suggesting that Johnson had a role in Kennedy's death. She claimed the idea came to her at a rally in which she inadvertently referred to Lady Bird Johnson as Lady MacBird, "and the whole thing just clicked." What began as a skit evolved into a full-length play, selling half a million printed copies.

Keach, just 25 when he portrayed the 65-year-old president, explained in a *New York Times* essay how he went about it: "I listened to hours of Johnson on tape and really nailed his accent and his cadences, aided by all my summers spent in Texas." With prop glasses, a false nose and body padding, "I wanted people to realize I was not 65, so I played MacBird with great physicality, climaxing with a spectacular fall to the deck for my death. I was enamored of the techniques I'd just learned studying in London, so I devised a straightforward fall, clutching my chest, saying, 'My heart, my heart' and going down hard. My elbows still hurt from doing it every night, but it was worth the pain to jolt the audience like that." (Lyndon Johnson died of a heart attack four years after the play closed.)

Some critics said the whole thing was too painful for such satire; more than one labeled the anti-war message in "MacBird!" as un-American. However, Peter Brook of Britain's Royal Shakespeare Company had a different take, writing that America is "the only land in the world where accusations like 'MacBird' could be heard on a public stage." One month after the New

York premiere, *Life* magazine said Garson had written a "little skit that grew too big for its britches" and had become "one of the oddest wonders of the American stage."

"MacBird!" had 386 performances in New York, then ran for several weeks at The Committee's theater in San Francisco. However, plans for a wider tour were scrubbed a few months later when Robert Kennedy (played in "MacBird!" by William Devane) was assassinated in Los Angeles.

◆ ◆ ◆

AS VIETNAM PROTESTS INCREASED it became clear that Johnson's quest for a second full term would face opposition from within his own party, led by the war's most vocal critic, Sen. Eugene McCarthy of Minnesota. I saw this first hand at a January, 1968 McCarthy rally in Iowa, where my father, Allen Funt, along with singer John Denver, entertained a crowd of enthusiastic McCarthy supporters. While passion for McCarthy was evident that night, contempt for Johnson was even clearer. Gallup polling during a six-week period from late January to March, showed approval of Johnson's Vietnam policies dropping from 40 percent to 26. At that point, Sen. Robert Kennedy of New York announced that he, too, would seek the nomination. And, as if things weren't bad enough for LBJ, he was now coming under constant fire from two brothers who presided over a prime-time series on CBS.

Tom and Dick Smothers gained popularity doing a non-political, non-controversial act that mixed folk songs with harmless banter ("Mom always liked you best"). When they landed on CBS in February of 1967 with "The Smothers Brothers Comedy Hour," they were viewed by network programmers as a safe bet, not as activists who would eventually help topple a president...

DICK: *Hey Tom, you know, I just read in the newspaper this week where President Johnson has now asked Congress to pass a series of taxes, you know, to discourage people from traveling abroad. What do you think about that?*

TOM: *I read that, too, but I don't think he has to go that far. I don't think that's necessary to go that far with it.*

DICK: *Well, look, it's a very, very, very, very difficult situation. You know, people keep spending money abroad, and it's hurting our economy. People keep wanting to travel to other countries instead of staying here in the United States.*

TOM: *Yeah, well, I think President Johnson should come up with something positive as an inducement to keep the people here, something very positive as an inducement to keep the people...*

DICK: *Yeah, that's right. That's good thinking. But, look, what can the president do to make people want to stay in this country?*

TOM: *Well, he could quit.*

Tom and Dick grew increasingly political on CBS, hiring several writers from The Committee to spoof the war, the president and his family. Johnson's daughters, Linda Bird and Luci Baines, were known to be fans of the "The Smothers Brothers," but they were reportedly saddened when David Frye, playing

LBJ, referred to his "semi-beautiful daughters."

In another sketch the actor Jim Backus ("Mr. Magoo," "Gilligan's Island") portrayed LBJ. (This created an odd bit of TV trivia: It was Backus who four years earlier had introduced Vaughn Meader and his JFK impersonation to the nation on "Talent Scouts.") The piece, titled "One Man's Country," had Backus, who looked a bit like Johnson, wearing a "Hail to the Chef" apron as he whipped up "secret" barbecue sauce. While the sauce was extra spicy, the sketch was rather mild compared to other material on "The Smothers Brothers" show, yet it hit a nerve at the White House. Johnson placed a middle-of-the-night call to CBS Chairman William Paley, after which Paley reportedly asked the brothers to "ease up" on LBJ. Instead, they pushed even harder.

During his '68 campaign Johnson grew despondent. "How is it possible," Doris Kearns Goodwin quotes him as asking, "that all these people could be so ungrateful to me after I had given them so much?" In a televised speech on March 31 that started out as a routine review of Vietnam developments, Johnson shocked the nation by announcing: "I shall not seek, and will not accept, the nomination of my party for another term as your President."

Without Johnson to harangue, the Smothers Brothers engineered their own fake presidential campaign with series regular Pat Paulsen posing as a candidate from the Straight Talking American Government Party (STAG). In what proved to be prescient—particularly in the Trump years—Paulson pledged to rely upon "outright lies, double talk and unfounded attacks" on opponents. His trademark rebuttal when challenged: "Picky, picky, picky."

The Smothers Brothers, meanwhile, engaged in renewed disagreements with CBS and its censors (more about which in the following chapter).

Pat Paulsen, like Democrat Hubert Humphrey, failed to win the election on November 5. Four days later, Lyndon Johnson wrote to the Smothers Brothers:

> *To be genuinely funny at a time when the world is in crisis is a task that would tax the talents of a genius; to be consistently questioned demands the wisdom of a saint.*
>
> *It is part of the price of leadership of this great and free nation to be the target of clever satirists. You have given the gift of laughter to our people. May we never grow so somber or self-important that we fail to appreciate the humor in our lives.*
>
> *If ever an Emmy is awarded for graciousness, I will cast my vote for you.*

No president has expressed greater appreciation of presidential parody, and few presidents have appreciated it less than the man who would next occupy the Oval Office.

4 / I am the president, make no mistake about it

"For 16 years you've had a lot of fun. You've had an opportunity to attack me and I think I've given as good as I've taken. But as I leave you, just think how much you're going to be missing. You don't have Nixon to kick around anymore because, gentlemen, this is my last press conference." —Richard Nixon

Nixon's sour-grapes goodbye to reporters following his loss in California's 1962 gubernatorial election underscored why he was such a ripe target for comedians and impersonators. Miraculously, Nixon rose from the ashes six years later to become president. In a clever routine on "The Ed Sullivan Show" David Frye portrayed both Nixon and Lyndon Johnson at a press conference...

NIXON: *The next question from that old man over there.*
JOHNSON: *Mister President, please, give me something to do. To tell you the truth, my fellow Americans, I'm going bananas. ... Mister President, what are you going to do about unemployment?*
NIXON: *Well let me just say this. Most of my friends are*

working, let me just say that. I have a job. Make no mistake about it, I have a job. I am working, make no mistake about that. However, this is merely a stepping stone in my career. I will not give up until I become the governor of California!

With his well-crafted Nixon caricature—even more compelling than his Johnson—Frye emerged in the late sixties as the nation's most accomplished acting president. John Kennedy's accent had been relatively easy for impersonators and Johnson, too, had a distinctive regional intonation with his Texas drawl. Nixon, born in Yorba Linda, California, spoke without any geographic cues, although his low-octave, blustery delivery, coupled with shifting glances and awkward smiles, gave performers plenty to work with. Even before the Watergate scandal revealed his true character, Nixon's oily personality and total lack of charm translated well as comedy.

"I do Nixon not by copying his real actions but by feeling his attitude, which is that he cannot believe that he really is president," Frye told *Esquire.* "He's trying to convince himself when he says, 'I am the President!' And the moving eyes and tongue merely symbolize the way his mind is working."

◆ ◆ ◆

GROWING UP IN BROOKLYN in the 1930s, David Shapiro often chatted with neighbors by day, and by night imitated the way they talked, even the way they walked, to entertain his parents and sister. His father, who ran a janitorial service, was not keen on his son's showbiz aspirations and urged David to take a job with him, which he did briefly after college. In the

David Shapiro, 21, at his sister Ruth's wedding in 1954.

evenings David would perform for a few dollars at local clubs, doing impressions of oft-parodied Hollywood stars like Jimmy Stewart and Cary Grant. "Our home had one bathroom," his sister Ruth Welch told me, "and I could never get in there. David was always practicing his faces in the mirror. He worked at it for hours at a time." She describes an unhappy young man: shy and insecure. "He only grew to be five-foot, three inches. Everyone called him 'Shorty' and he hated it."

Changing his name to David Frye, he worked his way onto some small stages in Manhattan. At the Village Gate, where he was filling in for a regular in early 1966, a talent scout saw him do a few standard bits—but the imitation that went over best was Robert Kennedy, who at the time was a U.S. senator from New York, with a voice Frye claimed sounded like Bugs Bunny ("'What's up doc?' is my line!"). Frye was booked on "The Merv Griffin Show" and soon after that on numerous variety programs, where Nixon impressions became his specialty, leading to 11 guest appearances on "The Tonight Show" along with several spots on "The Ed Sullivan Show." Frye also created four Nixon-focused comedy albums: "I Am the President" (1969), "Radio Free Nixon" (1971), "Richard Nixon Superstar" (1971), and "Richard Nixon: A Fantasy" (1973). This body of work was notable for the precision of Frye's voice impressions as well as the comedy itself. Frye went beyond "The rub-bah swan is mine," and delivered actual humor. On one album Frye goes back to the day Nixon was born, when a pediatrician (played by Frye) exclaims, "I've never seen a newborn child with a five-o'clock shadow." The doctor confides to a friend, "I can't quite put my finger on it, but I just don't trust that baby."

Frye's drive, plus his lifelong insecurity, had him practicing impressions relentlessly. Before he went on, patrons at New York clubs would often hear "I am the president, make no mistake about it," echoing from a stall in the restroom. Steve Allen once noticed that as Frye sat on the "Tonight Show" couch he'd

David Frye as Richard Nixon on "The Ed Sullivan Show."

sneak looks at postage stamp-sized photos of the notables he was about to impersonate. "I find that by looking at pictures it helps me grasp the image of the person," explained Frye. "Maybe it's just a crutch, but I do find that it's like hearing their voices."

Frye's greatest political impact came during his appearances on "The Smothers Brothers Comedy Hour," where he first turned up in November, 1967—a year before Nixon was elected. With his black hair and sideburns cut shorter than in later years and dressed in a tuxedo that looked like it might have been his father's, Frye came across like a young teen, although at the time he was a few days short of his 34th birthday.

Frye's debut with Tom and Dick Smothers was a turning point in his career. After rattling off some fairly routine impressions, including Gregory Peck, Henry Fonda and William F. Buckley ("My tongue is so long I'm the only man who can seal an envelope after it's in the mailbox"), Frye darted into politics as Nixon:

I've got a great dilemma next year, in '68. I don't know whether to stay on the sidelines and watch the Republican Party go right down the drain, or to go in there and blow the whole thing myself.

Then he switched to Robert Kennedy:

Despite what you've heard, Lyndon Johnson and I are becoming like brothers. Cain and Abel. A lot of people say I don't like Lyndon Johnson. I worship the quicksand this man walks on.

Then he's Johnson:

Bobby Kennedy is a man of great promise. He promises this, he promises this, he promises this. I come here tonight with a heavy heart, and a lot of indigestion.

Concluding as LBJ:

Everybody likes me. All the polls say so. Now, if only the Smothers Brothers would leave me alone!

Frye's debut with Tom and Dick Smothers came at the start of a tumultuous period in politics. Within three months, Nixon announced he would run for president. Two months after that, Johnson withdrew. Less than three months later, Robert Kennedy was assassinated. And 12 months after Frye's appearance, Nixon was the president-elect.

Richard Nixon became integral to David Frye's career, which is to say his entire life—much as John Kennedy had been with Vaughn Meader.

John Byner recalls a private party in the late sixties: "Everyone was doing Nixon. And people at this affair are getting up and doing their thing. And I get up and I do a little Nixon. I'm going back down to the crowd and David Frye is sitting at a table and he stops me. He says, 'Hey, John, are you doing Nixon just because I do him?' I said, 'What! He's my president, too.'"

◆ ◆ ◆

THE SMOTHERS BROTHERS cared even less for Nixon than they did for Johnson, growing bolder in using their prime-time platform for dissent. This worried CBS executives and network sponsors. The 1967 episode cited above has two noticeable edits during Frye's remarks as Nixon, but there is no record that I could find concerning what was cut or why. Veteran TV critic David Bianculli, who wrote the definitive book about Tom and Dick Smothers, "Dangerously Funny," explains that the

"Comedy Hour" episodes were heavily scrutinized by the Nixon White House and by CBS's Standards and Practices Department. A few weeks after Nixon's election in '68, Frye appeared as Sir Richard and was crowned King Richard as a chorus of townsfolk sang: "Rejoice, rejoice, there's no other choice...For now, he's the best we could find..."

In April of 1969, just three months after Nixon took office, CBS abruptly canceled the "Comedy Hour." Its stated excuse was that producers had failed to deliver an advance tape of a sensitive segment in a timely fashion. Tom Smothers later claimed the network had killed the show under pressure from the Nixon Administration.

Bianculli writes that he was unable to find a "smoking gun connecting Richard Nixon to the demise of [the show]." It was later revealed, however, by *Washington Post* reporters Bob Woodward and Carl Bernstein that Nixon's campaign funds were used to pay for a private investigation of the brothers. Also, in early 1970 Tom and Dick came under investigation by the IRS.

Meanwhile, the Smothers sued CBS for breach of contract. A jury found in their favor and ordered CBS to pay $776,000 plus an additional $140,000 for a copyright violation—but the sum was far less than the brothers had sought.

Even without their network TV platform, the Smothers Brothers continued seeking ways to confront the Nixon Administration. One project, an offbeat 1972 theatrical motion picture titled "Another Nice Mess," proved to be a financial fiasco, a creative flop and quite a mess in its own right. Yet, it is a fascinating example of presidential mimicry with a rich backstory that was all but lost for a half century until film buffs located a print and determined that the property had slipped into public domain.

Produced by Tom Smothers under a banner he called SMOBRO International Productions, Inc., the 66-minute movie looks like something created under the influence of hallucinogens which, considering lifestyles in the early '70s, might be the best explanation for a film that ran only briefly in theaters and grossed just $30,000 before being locked away by Tom Smothers, who dismissed it as "terrible." Written and directed by Bob Einstein (best known for creating the character Super Dave Osborn, and for playing the lovable Funhouser on "Curb Your Enthusiasm," as well as for being the brother of actor Albert Brooks), it starred Rich Little, the nation's hottest impersonator, as Nixon, along with character actor Herb Voland as Vice President Spiro Agnew. In this twisted farce, "Nixon" and "Agnew"

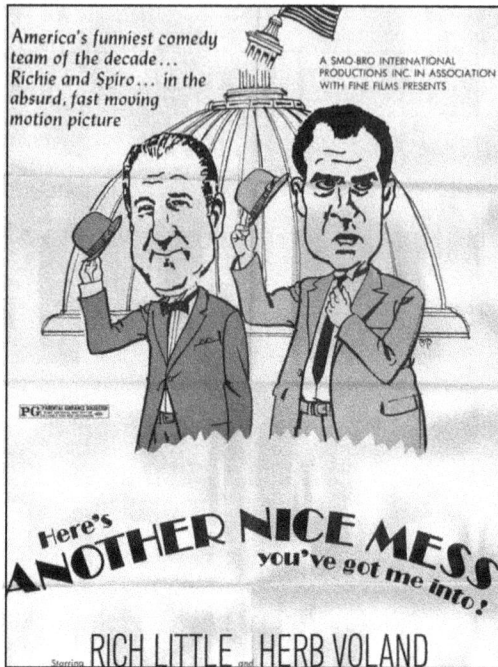

America's funniest comedy team of the decade... Richie and Spiro... in the absurd, fast moving motion picture

A SMO-BRO INTERNATIONAL PRODUCTIONS INC. IN ASSOCIATION WITH FINE FILMS PRESENTS

PG

Here's ANOTHER NICE MESS you've got me into!

Starring RICH LITTLE and HERB VOLAND

are depicted as Stan Laurel and Oliver Hardy, but there are also scenes in which Little plays President Nixon as himself, breaking the fourth wall to tell viewers how bad the film is. Adding to the confusion, vintage clips of the real Laurel and Hardy are interspersed, as if to suggest they are eavesdropping on the action.

The film opens with the inauguration outside the Capitol, as Agnew pulls a thread from Nixon's pants, causing them to fall off. Things only get stranger as an elderly Adolf Hitler turns up at the White House, wearing an Hawaiian shirt while working as a spy for the Chinese government. None other than Steve Martin makes his film debut as a long-haired hippie whose entire dialogue consists of the words, "Well, actually, I was walking by over here, and..."

Several published reports suggest that Nixon got word of the film during its production phase and arranged a drug raid on the California home of Tom Smothers. Nothing was found because insiders alerted Smothers, and by the time the police arrived his premises had been carefully cleansed.

Meanwhile, in the finished film, Rich Little as Nixon gives viewers a message:

> *My fellow Americans, as you know I am a great supporter of the motion picture industry. Make no mistake about that. But I urge you not to see a picture called "Another Nice Mess." It ridicules the American way of life.*

As if the Smothers Brothers' filmic assault on Nixon wasn't enough, he was mocked in another movie at about the same time, this one written and produced by a Frenchman named Bertrand Castelli and his wife, Lorees Yerby. "Richard," ostensibly tells Nixon's life story, using old newsreels and TV clips, plus an impersonation by the actor James La Roe, who used the stage name Richard M. Dixon because he bore an uncanny resemblance to the 37th president. During Nixon's reign, Dixon was in demand for cameos on "Laugh-In" as well as on talk programs hosted by Johnny Carson, Merv Griffin and Mike Douglas. In "Richard," Dixon has what *The New York Times* critic called "one lovely sequence," where he walks on stage, having been introduced as the world's most powerful man, and breaks into a clumsy vaudeville dance. It's "almost horribly appealing," wrote Roger Greenspun. "It is a fine moment, worth waiting for—but, alas, it comes in the first three minutes of an 83-minute movie, and the rest goes downhill."

While Dixon was doing Nixon as a vaudevillian, Howard Hesseman took a similar approach on The Committee stage in San Francisco. "We called it 'Nixon Laughs'" recalls producer Alan Myerson. "It was inspired by the common belief that Richard Nixon was an uptight humorless, if dangerous, clod. The scene had Nixon (Hesseman) in his office as one of his toadies introduced a burlesque comic (Jim Cranna) to try to loosen him up by teaching him how to be funny. It concluded with Nixon hitting himself over the head with a rubber chicken."

♦ ♦ ♦

SOON AFTER THE '72 ELECTION, Nixon threw a party at his home in San Clemente, California, to thank the many celebrities who had supported him in his landslide win over Democrat George McGovern. While today's Hollywood crowd generally favors progressive politics, the creative community in Nixon's

Nixon meets Rich Little in San Clemente.

day was quite conservative. Yet, many of Nixon's pre-Watergate accomplishments were surprisingly liberal. Attending the party were Jack Benny, John Wayne, George Burns, Debbie Reynolds and dozens of others including Rich Little, whose appearance in "Another Nice Mess" had gone so totally unnoticed that he was able to comfortably rub Republican shoulders at poolside. Little was introduced to the president, and Reynolds urged him to do the Nixon imitation he had been performing on Ed Sullivan's show. Reluctant at first, Little finally puffed his cheeks and switched to his Nixon voice: "Mister President, let me make this perfectly clear. This is a wonderful party you're throwing, and I'm thrilled to be here. Make no mistake about that." Guests wondered if it was permissible to laugh, and Nixon looked puzzled; he had no idea who Little was and couldn't place the voice. As Little recalls: "Nixon was glaring at me. Then he turned to his wife, Pat, and said, 'Why is this young man speaking in such a strange voice?'" When it was over, John Wayne shouted, "Somebody get a rope!"

Rich Little has the distinction of having performed impressions of every president from Kennedy to Biden. Born in Ottawa, Canada, he never worked at the counterculture venues in Greenwich Village or with improv groups in Chicago and San Francisco. His first shot on American TV was on Judy Garland's Hollywood-based variety show. Little was a lifelong Republican, a credential which, as we'll see later, made him a rarity among presidential impersonators and allowed him unique access at 1600 Pennsylvania Avenue—at least when a Republican was in residence.

Little owes much of his early success to Ed Sullivan. In

his memoir he writes that he never cared for Sullivan personally, though like many performers in the sixties he was careful
not to offend TV's most powerful star-maker. According to the
book, Little's first appearance on "The Ed Sullivan Show" included an epic introduction by the easily-tongue-tied host: "Ladies
and gentlemen, I'd like to bring out a young imper...impro...pro...
per...comic, who comes to us from beautiful downtown Canada,
making his very first appearance here on our show. Let's have a
big U.S. welcome for Little Richard!"

Makes a wonderful story. However, in a 1973 appearance
on the "Tonight Show," Little said, "You know the first show I
ever did with (Sullivan), he gave me a great build up: 'A young
impersonator from Canada, a fine youngster, so welcome out
here, Buddy Rich!'"

That's why comedians are hard to take seriously.

◆ ◆ ◆

AS THE WATERGATE STORY UNFOLDED, some of the
most effective Nixon-bashing occurred on radio. Ground zero
was at KRLA, an AM station in Los Angeles that helped pioneer a
type of "newscast" in which fact blended with comedy. The writ-
er-performers came to be known as The Credibility Gap, whose
members changed over time but notably included David Land-
er and Michael McKean (later Lenny and Squiggy in the sitcom
"Laverne & Shirley"), and a 26-year-old former child actor
named Harry Shearer, who portrayed Nixon. Though Shearer
went on to an eclectic career encompassing almost every form
of media, Nixon became his obsession.

Shearer grew up in L.A., taking piano lessons at age four

from a woman named Hazel McMillan. "I was a recalcitrant prac-
ticer," he recalls, "and so, whether it was because of that or other
reasons, Mrs. McMillan decided to change careers and became
a talent agent for children." She got Shearer an audition for Jack
Benny's show, the result of which was an eight-year stint with
the legendary comic on both radio and TV. Another regular on
Benny's programs was Mel Blanc, best known as the man behind the voices of popular cartoon characters including Bugs
Bunny and Daffy Duck. Blanc befriended Shearer, who years later would become the voice of dozens of animated characters on
"The Simpsons," including C. Montgomery Burns, Ned Flanders
and Principal Skinner.

In the mid-60s KRLA was the number two rock-music
station in L.A., behind powerhouse KHJ. Seeking an edge, KRLA
turned to comedy news. Shearer recorded an audition—doing
the voice of Nixon's 1968 opponent Hubert Humphrey—and
was hired and on the air the following day.

Speaking to me from his home in New Orleans, Shearer
recounted how his interest in Nixon developed. For him, playing
the part was not so much about one-liners and Ed Sullivan-style
schtick. It was political, and personal.

"I was motivated by more than creative interest because
I was still in my twenties and had just gotten out of the six-year
purgatory of having my ass hauled to Vietnam, and I had a lin-
gering loathing for these guys who were running this particular
war. By that point it was possible to know that the war had a
fraudulent basis. So I had great motivation to be doing Nixon."

After a year on KRLA, The Credibility Gap moved to
KPPC-FM, trading three 10-minute shows per day for a single

15-minute broadcast. While Shearer was doing his Nixon for a relatively small Southern California radio audience, David Frye was dominating the national television scene. "As I got into it more thoughtfully at KPPC," Shearer explains, "I'd be aware of those other guys and thought they were kind of gimmicky— emphasizing the jolliness of the delivery, in the case of David Frye. I wanted to get into Nixon's head a little more."

By the mid-70s The Credibility Gap had left KPPC and taken its sketches on the road, performing in clubs and concert venues. The day Nixon quit, August 8, 1974, the group went on stage, with Shearer sitting on the floor as Nixon, putting trophies in a box and singing "The party's over..." In fact, for Shearer's career doing Nixon the party had only begun.

◆ ◆ ◆

HARRY SHEARER'S LENGTHY RESUME includes two stints as a writer and performer on "Saturday Night Live" as well as hilarious collaborations with Christopher Guest, Rob Reiner and Michael McKean in mockumentaries, the first and most notable of which is 1984's send up of a fictional rock band, "This Is Spinal Tap." A year before the film's release, Shearer launched a weekly radio program called "Le Show" which, as of this writing, is in its 40th year. *Vogue* magazine described it as a "wildly clever, iconoclastic stew of talk, music, political commentary, readings of inadvertently funny public documents or trade magazines and scripted skits."

"Le Show" persists in reminding listeners what a truly despicable character Nixon was, primarily through a recurring bit called "Nixon in Heaven." Shearer says it's based on two dubious assumptions: (1) that there is a heaven, and (2) that Richard Nixon, after spending time in hell, managed to get in. In one episode, taking place during the final days of Donald Trump's presidency, Nixon asks chief of staff H.R. Haldeman: "If I said 'law and order president,' whose name would you associate with that phrase?" Nixon is miffed because Trump covets that title, but Haldeman comforts Nixon by reminding him, "You're the Marlboro Man of law-and-order presidents. It's as if some other cigarette company has a cowboy in their ad, but everybody knows it's the Marlboro Man, right?"

"A severe distaste for the man made me want to penetrate him psychologically," says Shearer, leading to a more nuanced impersonation. A breakthrough in the process came in 1992 when historian Stanley Kutler sued the government for the release of more than 3,000 hours of recordings made during Nixon's presidency. As a result, a trove of material was made public beginning in 1996, and soon Shearer was taking frequent trips to a warehouse outside Washington, DC, where he'd put on headphones and listen to Nixon tapes. "I had no plan professionally," he explains. "It was just, oh my god, this is amazing stuff."

Along the way Shearer met Kutler, and the two Nixon buffs agreed to collaborate on a television series, using actual dialogue from the tapes. Shearer, who has a home in London, sold the six-part series to Britain's Sky TV. Shearer plays Nixon, with a cast of other actors playing his associates. The dialogue is precisely what was said on the tapes, nothing else. But Shearer's concept is to imagine what things would look like had Nixon hidden cameras as well as audio recorders in the Oval Office. The result isn't so much funny as it is intriguing, and historically profound. Titled "Nixon's the One"—his campaign slogan in '68—the series examines what Shearer calls Nixon's "bizarre and remarkable unintentional humor."

"Nixon was determined to cast almost a hyper-masculine image to his persona. He would go out of his way to utter a pretty safe profanity, you know (switches to Nixon voice), 'God damn those people!' as if to show he was a real man. There was deliberate flaunting of a kind of garden variety profanity. But then I noticed that he had mannerisms that were at odds with that—he'd flutter his eyelashes when he was emphasizing a thought, or his hands would fly upwards and outwards in almost a butterfly motion. And he'd purse his lips in thought, but it looked as if he was checking his lipstick. It was so at odds with how he wanted to depict himself that I felt I had to nail that."

Shearer says he picked Sky believing that British TV executives were less likely to interfere with the creative process than their American counterparts. Still, why the 2013 series was never picked up in the U.S. by, say, HBO or Showtime, defies explanation (it can be found on YouTube and some on-demand download sites). In Shearer's view, "Nixon was one of the great comic figures of the 20th century."

◆ ◆ ◆

WHILE HARRY SHEARER'S ROBUST CAREER has stretched far beyond his infatuation with Nixon, David Frye's professional world collapsed when Nixon resigned in disgrace, much as Vaughn Meader spiraled to oblivion almost immediately after the Kennedy assassination. Appearing in Cleveland the night after Nixon quit, Frye's first line was, "There goes my act." Two months later Frye made his last appearance on "The Tonight Show," never getting booked on latenight television again. He released two more albums focusing on the presidency: "David Frye Presents the Big Debate" (1980) and "Clinton: An Oral History" (1998) but audiences who welcomed his LBJ and roared at his Nixon no longer seemed interested. Off stage, his sour attitude irked showbiz colleagues. Journalist Phil Berger, who studied stand-up comics, described Frye as "a dark, brooding figure, whose moods capsized in a shot glass." A reporter for the *San Francisco Chronicle*, John Wasserman, wrote about how Frye was fired from a gig at the Fairmont Hotel for being "drunk as a skunk."

"The nightlife became too much for him," Frye's sister Ruth Welch told me. "He died penniless (in 2011). By then I didn't even know where he was living; my birthday cards were returned.

"One night I was cooking dinner and I received a phone call from the coroner in Las Vegas informing me that David had been found dead in his apartment. I was told he suffered a heart attack.

"He was very generous with me, but he pissed most of his money away, just as he did with his career."

◆ ◆ ◆

FOOTNOTE: A few years after Nixon resigned, I found myself standing next to him on a line at the post office on Second Avenue in Manhattan. He was wearing an ill-fitting tan raincoat, and I struggled to avoid staring at the black hairs growing atop his nose. He was accompanied by two very hard-to-miss Secret

Service agents.

I introduced myself, and Nixon explained that he was mailing his income taxes, "something I always like to do in person." He did not say, "Make no mistake about it." However, his voice sounded just like Rich Little's, his expression was precisely David Frye's, and his dainty gestures were exactly as described by Harry Shearer. Even in licking a stamp, he seemed easy to dislike.

Not long after that I attended a business conference in Phoenix where I spoke at some length with Nixon's successor, a pleasant fellow. He was nothing at all like the crazy characterizations of him that had been widely seen on TV—portrayals that would eventually chase him from office.

5 / I'm Gerald Ford and you're not

G erald Ford's presidency began in 1974 with a haunting-ly controversial move: "a full, free, and absolute pardon unto Richard Nixon for all offenses against the United States." It ended just two years later with a loss at the polls to a relatively unknown former governor and peanut farmer, Jimmy Carter of Georgia. Ford was a decent man, who served as both vice president and president without being elected to either post. He will best be remembered—at least within these pag-es—as the first sitting president to be impersonated on NBC's "Saturday Night Live."

Ford referred to the Nixon saga as "a long national night-mare," and defended his pardon as a means of speeding the country's healing process. The decision unquestionably hurt Ford with voters in the '76 election, though many historians have since concluded that the pardon was a wise, even heroic decision. Making matters worse for Ford were the images of him cultivated on SNL: a klutz with modest intellect. Neither depic-tion was true.

A football star at the University of Michigan, Ford earned a law degree at Yale and served as a lieutenant commander in the Navy. He represented Michigan's 5th Congressional District in the House of Representatives for 25 years, nine of them as nMinority Leader. When Spiro Agnew resigned as Nixon's vice president in 1973, charged with tax evasion and money laundering, Ford was overwhelmingly approved by the House and Senate as his replacement. Eight months later, Nixon resigned, making Gerald Ford the 38th president.

Just over a year into Ford's presidency, SNL had its premiere, on October 11, 1975. Chevy Chase anchored "Weekend Update" that first night, rattling off a series of jokes at Ford's expense, among them a new campaign slogan: "If he's so dumb, how come he's president?"

Three weeks later, with the writers looking for a cold open, Chase volunteered to play Ford in a sketch. He said he'd do it without trying to look or sound like the president; he'd just bumble and stumble.

ANNOUNCER DON PARDO: *Ladies and gentlemen, the president of the United States.*

[MUSIC: Hail to the Chief. Chase enters and becomes tangled with the American flag on stage. He drops his papers, then moves behind podium.]

CHASE: *My fellow Americans, ladies and gentlemen, members of the press, and my immediate family. First, may I thank you all for being here, and I am, and my immediate family. First, may I thank you all for being here, and I am and my immediate family. Thank you all for being here. And I am truly honored to be asked by you to open the 'Saturday Night' show with Harvey Cosell.*

[He pours water into a glass, then picks up an empty glass and attempts to drink from it.]

CHASE: *I do have two major announcements to make…*

[He stumbles and falls.]

CHASE: *Whoops! Uh, oh.*

[Gets up.]

CHASE: *No problem. No problem. Okay.*

"Ford" tries to drink more water, this time from the empty pitcher. He bangs his head on the podium, stumbles to the floor a second time, and then hurts his hand pounding the podium. He walks stage right, trips over two folding chairs and, sprawled on the floor, says to camera: "Live from New York, it's Saturday Night!"

◆ ◆ ◆

SNL'S BACKSTORY stretches more than a year—from summer of '74 until the premiere in fall of '75—and varies depending on who is telling it and whose memory you trust. What's certain is that credit for the show goes primarily to four men: Herb Schlosser, the NBC president; Dick Ebersol, an ABC sports executive who was lured by Schlosser to run late-night at NBC; Lorne Michaels, the young Canadian visionary hired by Ebersol to produce his new series, and Johnny Carson, NBC's King of Late-Night.

Carson had been doing his highly successful "Tonight Show" five nights a week, with a rerun on Saturday. He notified NBC that he no longer wanted reruns on weekends, insisting they be slotted on occasional weeknights so he could take more time off. That left a void on Saturday night. "I wanted to do the show live if possible," recalled Schlosser, "and I wanted to do it in New York City, because New York had lost all of its entertainment shows. Everything had moved to Burbank. Even Carson had moved to Burbank."

Lorne Michaels said he wanted the new show to be "cool." In his initial view, "This was taking the sensibilities that were in music, stage, and the movies and bringing them to television."

Numerous formats were considered. One of the more intriguing twists, at least in terms of presidential impersonations, was the notion of having Rich Little as permanent host. Little was under contract to NBC at the time and was widely considered to be the most renowned impersonator of the day. During Chase's second sketch as Ford, text at the bottom of the screen declared: THIS IS NOT A GOOD IMPRESSION OF GERALD FORD. BUT RICH LITTLE WON'T WORK FOR SCALE.

Imagine how different SNL might have been in its formative years with Little, a conservative, as host. Would he have played Gerald Ford in the style that Chevy Chase ultimately became famous for? Would he have handled the Richard Nixon portrayal with the edge crafted by Dan Aykroyd? We'll never know because Michaels was dead set against Little. As he told Tom Shales and James Andrew Miller in the book "Live from New York," "In the seventies, I was much more proud of who I wouldn't allow on the show—people who had just been all over Las Vegas and prime-time television." Although Michaels described some of them as "really great," he insisted that "any association with the Rich Littles and the John Byners and the original 'Tonight Show' guys like Dayton Allen would have been antithetical to what I was trying to do."

So Michaels and Ebersol assembled a cast of relatively unknown performers, dubbed by veteran writer Herb Sargent— the only member of the writing staff over 40—the "Not Ready for Prime Time Players." Sargent had a previous credit that was especially important as SNL developed its spoofs of politicians and the presidency: He had been a producer on the American version of "That Was the Week That Was."

The first cast member signed was Gilda Radner, 28, followed a few months later by John Belushi, 26, Dan Aykroyd and Laraine Newman, both 23. Chevy Chase, 31, initially turned down a writing job but later came aboard when given both writing and performing credits. This troupe of unknowns grew out of Michaels' determination to find exciting new talent, but also because NBC's budget was quite low, even by TV standards in the mid-'70s. Michaels had about $134,000 per week to play with. He paid cast performers $750 per show, with writers getting weekly paychecks ranging from $350 to a top of $650. To lure a staff, Michaels promised to change television's pattern of giving talent high pay but little creative freedom. SNL would deliver just the opposite: low pay in return for considerable freedom.

Originally called "Saturday Night" (because ABC had a show with Howard Cosell titled "Saturday Night Live") the NBC series broke new ground in television and almost immediately established a formula for imitating and mocking sitting presidents. "All the established order had been overturned," Michaels recalls of the time. "The war and Watergate and the recession of the early '70s, everything was being questioned. And distrust of authority was just in the air."

◆ ◆ ◆

ALAN ZWEIBEL was only 24, working by day at a delicatessen in Queens, N.Y., and hitching rides into Manhattan with his friend Billy Crystal at night, to do standup at the comedy club known as Catch a Rising Star. One night, as it neared 1 a.m., Zweibel sat at the bar waiting for Crystal to finish his act, when a stranger sat down next to him and volunteered, "You're one of the worst comics I've ever seen, but your material isn't bad. Did you write it?" That was how Alan Zweibel met Lorne Michaels. A few days later they had a formal interview at the Plaza Hotel and Zweibel handed over a folder with more than a thousand jokes. Michaels read just one:

The post office is about to issue a stamp commemorating prostitution in the United States. It's a ten-cent stamp. If you want to lick it, it's a quarter.

That was in May. On July 7, 1975, Zweibel along with nine other writers and various cast members arrived on the 17th floor of the RCA Building at Rockefeller Center for their first day of work on "Saturday Night Live." As the room filled with the likes of Belushi, Aykroyd, Newman and Chase, Zweibel became so nervous that he crouched behind a potted plant.

"First show, Alan?" asked a woman, poking her head through the leaves. "Yes," he said. "How did you know my name's Alan?"

Gilda Radner's reply, "You're the only one wearing a name tag."

Three months later, Chevy Chase anchored the first "Weekend Update," and used the joke about the prostitution

Alan Zweibel, front, with the original SNL writing staff, from left: Rosie Shuster (Mrs. Lorne Michaels), Tom Schiller, Anne Beatts and Michael O'Donoghue.

stamp, marking the start of Zweibel's robust career. [Remarkably, the same exact joke was used again the following season when Jane Curtin anchored "Update."] When I spoke with Zweibel for this book he had just finished his memoir, "Laugh Lines: My Life Helping Funny People Be Funnier." He'd won several Emmys and Writers Guild awards for his work on "It's Garry Shandling's Show" and "Curb Your Enthusiasm," picked up a Tony for "700 Sundays" with Billy Crystal, and written a bestseller about his close friend Gilda Radner, who died of cancer in 1989.

I asked about the political game plan at SNL in those early days.

"Don't forget how young we all were. Nixon had resigned and Ford had just replaced him. We were of an age where the Republicans were the bad guys. And we felt that we were punching up, so to speak, which is really part of any political satire. It's the little guy taking a shot at the guy above him. [Monty] Python did it. Go all the way back to Jonathan Swift. That's the nature of satire. So it was never a declaration, but given our individual politics—Ford comes along, this guy who not only pardoned Nixon, but kept falling down a lot, so, you know, the comedy just seemed like a natural thing to do."

Was the staff entirely liberal?

"I'm going to say flat out, there were no Republicans."

♦ ♦ ♦

CHEVY CHASE WAS SKILLED AT PRATFALLS, so much so that during SNL's first season he did "the fall" to open almost every show, beginning with the second episode. On the fourth show, November 8, he did one as Ford and it stuck. (It wasn't as easy as it looked. In one sketch Chase tumbled over a podium, which was supposed to have been padded but wasn't, and suffered an injury to his testicles, causing Chase to spend a week in the hospital and two weeks off the show.)

The Christmas program in '75 featured Chase's best Ford. Ready to trim the White House tree, he's singing a carol to the tune of "Easter Parade"... the butler (Garrett Morris) enters with a drink...

MORRIS: *Here is your cognac, Mister President.*
CHASE: *Fred, you've been with me a long time now. I don't think on Christmas eve you have to call me Mister President any more.*
MORRIS: *Ah, Mister President, my name is Frank.*
CHASE: *Frank...*
MORRIS: *Uh huh. What should I call you?*
CHASE: *Well, how about Doctor President.*

Morris extends a silver tray with the drink... Chase

Chase as Ford on SNL in 1975.

takes the tray, so Morris downs the drink. After several more mishaps, including Chase hanging stockings
above the fireplace upside down, he climbs a ladder to
place the final ornament atop the tree ... falls, and he
and the tree crash to the ground. Chase turns and says:
"Live from New York, it's Saturday Night!"

Alan Zweibel marvels at how the most significant political impersonation since Vaughn Meader's JFK was done without any attempt to look or sound like the president. "I think the
fun was, Chevy would look like Chevy. He'd do what Chevy does,
and say that he was President Ford. And it was just accepted. It
was revolutionary, when you think about it, because the predecessors, including Rich Little and all of them, when they would
impersonate a president, they would get applause based on the
proximity of how much they captured in terms of the voice. And
it was accompanied by a joke that was either good or bad. But
with Chevy, I don't remember one discussion where we said,

'Should we make him look like Ford or not?' If there was, it was in a room that I was not in."

◆ ◆ ◆

THE LOWEST PAID WRITERS that first season were Al Franken and Tom Davis. Like Zweibel, they were granted a waiver from the Writers Guild in order to be compensated at the below-scale rate of $350 per week and were called "apprentices." Franken and Davis, friends since high school, had been performing as a comedy duo in L.A. and agreed to share a single fee, each pocketing $175 a week to write for SNL.

Al Franken might be the single most qualified person to recount SNL's birth and to evaluate its decades-long political impact (more about which later). He wrote for SNL in two stints during the '70s and '80s, and then, in 2009, was elected to the U.S. Senate from Minnesota, serving until 2018 when dubious charges of sexual impropriety—subject to varied interpretation, including his own—led to a surprisingly abrupt resignation. When I spoke with him he was still bitter, but also comedically lighthearted about his experience, and politically diplomatic.

Franken was a political junkie even back in the mid-'70s, so during SNL's mid-season break he tagged along with friends to New Hampshire and rode the press bus for a few days in the run-up to the presidential primary. There he bumped into Ron Nessen, press secretary to Gerald Ford. "There was a big holding room for the press, and Nessen was there," Franken recalls. "I went up to him and he was very familiar with the show, although it hadn't been on very long. I asked him, I said, 'Well, would you like to host?' And he said, 'yeah.' When I got back I told Lorne and Lorne said, 'You know, I'm the producer.' And I go, 'Yeah, that's right.'"

Franken chuckles as he thinks back on his brazen offer to a top White House official and the quandary it created for both Gerald Ford and Lorne Michaels. The administration was uncertain about how to deal with the weekly humiliation Ford was suffering on SNL and the thought of allowing his press secretary to be a guest host didn't strike everyone at the White House as a smart plan. Michaels was also getting negative vibes from his staff, many of whom wondered if it was wise to invite a political operative into the henhouse. It's worth emphasizing the uncharted nature of all this: SNL was a new TV phenomenon and Ford was the first and only president it had ever spoofed. Ford had served less than one term and was struggling to remove Nixon's stain from the presidency while facing a challenge from Ronald Reagan for the GOP nomination. He wasn't the bumbler SNL made him out to be, but he was hardly Mister Charisma. Plus, there was no getting around the fact that he had, indeed, stumbled on the steps of Air Force One during a trip to Austria, and had several other unfortunate close calls.

Ford was planning to attend the annual Radio and Television Correspondents Dinner in March and intended to make a few, hopefully clever, remarks, as he had the year before. Word was passed by Ford's aides that Chevy Chase might make a good headliner for the event, and the invitation went out. Ford felt he had no choice but to meet the SNL problem head on, and a room filled with appreciative reporters would be a good place. "We all fell in love with Ford," recalled CBS correspondent Bob Schieffer, who covered Nixon and Ford, "because it has been so awful at

Chase, Michaels and Ford in Washington.

the White House for so long—and so mean."

Two days before the dinner Ford suffered a surprising loss to Ronald Reagan in the North Carolina primary, raising tension within the administration and adding weight to Ford's image problem. Black-tie-wearing guests at the Washington Hilton included Lorne Michaels and Herb Schlosser, the NBC president. Chase entered from the rear of the ballroom accompanied by John Belushi and Dan Aykroyd posing as Secret Service agents. After losing his way among the crowd Chase stumbled to the stage, banging his head on the podium. Surprisingly, that was about the only humorous thing in Chase's act. He gave an unfunny speech pretending to be Ford (referring to the swine flu outbreak: "I have also ordered that the state of North Carolina get the inoculations last.") Ford sat about ten feet to Chase's left, dutifully laughing when possible.

Though he wasn't much of a quipster, Ford had on his staff one of the top gag writers in show business, Robert Orbin, who had built a career writing jokes for TV performers as well as politicians from both parties. Orbin's script for Ford to read at the dinner, typed in a large, easy-to-read font, is preserved at the Ford Library. Its highlights include:

[WE OPEN WITH THE PRESIDENT PULLING
THE TABLECLOTH AS HE GOES TO THE LECTERN ...
APPROACHING WITH A SHEAF OF PAPERS IN ONE
HAND AND THE SPEECH BOOK IN THE OTHER.
PUTTING THE SHEAF OF PAPERS ON THE LECTERN,
HE LETS THEM CASCADE TO THE FLOOR AND
BEGINS WITH APLOMB...]
... GOOD EVENING. I'M GERALD FORD [POINTING
AT CHASE] AND YOU'RE NOT!
... I WANT TO COMMEND THE RADIO AND T.V.
CORRESPONDENTS' ASSOCIATION ON THEIR VERY
INTERESTING CHOICE OF MASTER OF CEREMONIES.
THAT'S ALL I NEED – NORTH CAROLINA AND CHEVY
CHASE IN THE SAME WEEK.
NO, I REALLY ENJOYED HIS FINE PERFORMANCE.
MR. CHEVY CHASE, YOU'RE A VERY, VERY FUNNY
SUBURB.
I DO APPRECIATE THE SATURDAY NIGHT SHOW
SENDING CHEVY CHASE TO WASHINGTON – AND IN
RETURN, ON APRIL 17th, WASHINGTON IS SENDING
THE SATURDAY NIGHT SHOW OUR VERY OWN RON

NESSEN TO BE THEIR GUEST HOST.

... NOW DON'T MISUNDERSTAND, I HAVE NOTHING AGAINST RON NESSEN BECOMING A PERFORMER. I LIKE SHOW BUSINESS. I LIKE THE PEOPLE IN SHOW BUSINESS. IN FACT, ALL MY LIFE I HAVE HAD NOTHING BUT RESPECT FOR SHOW BUSINESS PERSONALITIES. IT'S JUST THAT I WOULDN'T WANT MY DAUGHTER VOTING FOR ONE.

(Later, as he wraps up...)

... IN A WORLD THAT HAS SEEN THE GRADUAL SHRINKAGE IN MEDIA FREEDOMS, AMERICANS CAN TAKE HEART AND TAKE PRIDE IN THE FACT THAT OUR FREEDOMS HAVE ENDURED AND ARE STRONGER THAN EVER TODAY.

UNLIKE MOST EVERYTHING ELSE THAT HAS BEEN SAID TONIGHT, FREEDOM IS NO LAUGHING MATTER. THANK YOU AGAIN FOR LETTING ME SHARE THIS EVENING WITH YOU.

Energized by his boffo performance, Ford departed and, despite the late hour, took a 20-minute swim in the White House pool.

◆ ◆ ◆

GUEST HOSTS AT SNL usually spend a full week preparing, but Ron Nessen arrived just two days before his April 17 gig. Having worked for 12 years at NBC News, he knew his way around the building, but what went on inside Studio 8H—including copious drug use ("We need it to stay awake" was the standard explanation)—was new to him. Bob Orben had tried to dissuade Nessen from appearing on SNL. As Orben recounted for University of Missouri researchers years later, "When Ron first said he was gonna do 'Saturday Night Live,' I said, 'Don't do it, Ron,' and he said, 'I have script control.' and all that. I said, 'You have nothing. This (Washington) is your ballpark and this (New York) is their ballpark and it's not good." SNL writer Tom Davis recalled, "We were amazed that with Chevy's handle on Ford that Nessen would agree to appear."

The show began with a nonpolitical cold open, but the "Live from New York..." line was delivered on tape by Ford himself, recorded in the Oval Office. It was stiff, dry and completely humorless. After Don Pardo's opening voiceover, Ford says, "Ladies and gentlemen, the press secretary to the President of the United States." By now if viewers were laughing at all, it was probably at Ford, not with him. Nessen takes the stage in a pale blue three-piece suit. Describing his daily responsibilities, he explains, "I've learned a few phrases to make my job easier. Phrases like, 'What the president really said was...' or, 'What the president really meant was...' or, 'What the president really bumped into was...' or, 'What the president mispronounced was...'" Nessen goes on to review what he's learned at the White House, including such things as, "How to remove a necktie from a helicopter rotor blade while (Ford's) still wearing it." The show had been on for barely six of its 90 minutes, but several things were already clear: (1) Ron Nessen seemed to be as big a self-promoter as Chevy Chase, (2) Rather than refuting SNL's insults about the president, thanks to Nessen they were all being confirmed, and (3) defeating Jimmy Carter in November would be exceedingly difficult.

The show included a few more damaging bits, including an Oval Office spoof with Chase as Ford and Nessen as himself. For the most part, Nessen watched as Chase did his best demeaning nonsense, such as hitting golf balls with a tennis racquet and stabbing his neck with a letter opener.

Interviewed in *Playboy*, SNL writer Michael O'Donoghue described the episode: "Nessen did it to co-opt us and we did it to co-opt him, so that was a trade-off." SNL writer Rosie Shuster said she and her colleagues agreed, "The president's watching. Let's make him cringe and squirm."

"Ultimately," Al Franken told me, "the president and his kids were not happy with that show at all. And falling out of favor with the family and the president is not a good thing for the press secretary."

♦ ♦ ♦

I'M NOT GIVING AWAY THE ENDING by mentioning here that Gerald Ford lost the election in '76 and Chevy Chase quit SNL for the greener film lots in Hollywood. (He did stick around for the start of SNL's groundbreaking second season.) Chase was bitter about his year at SNL, lashing out in later interviews about the cast and crew. A writer for the *Washington Post*, Geoff Edgers, visited him in 2018 and concluded: "Chase can be arrogant, unpredictable and mean. He is a masterful put-down artist. He can be blunt or tone-deaf, depending on what he fesses up to, and he doesn't always seem to understand the fine line between comic provocation and publicity disaster.

"But Chase can also be hilarious, sensitive and surprisingly supportive. Sometimes, he's all of these things at once."

Looking back at SNL's debut season and its first attempt at presidential parody, it appears that while viewers learned little about the real Gerald Ford, they learned even less about the real Chevy Chase.

For his part, Ford was never bitter, at least publicly. Seven years after he left office I spent an evening with him and a few dozen other guests at a party in Phoenix. I found him to be somewhat dull, but cordial and considerate to a fault. He never misspoke—and he didn't trip over anything. In his autobiography, "A Time to Heal," Ford wrote: "The news coverage was harmful ... But even more damaging was the fact that Johnny Carson and Chevy Chase used my missteps for their jokes." He added, "Their antics—and I'll admit that I laughed at them myself—helped create a public perception of me as a stumbler. And that wasn't funny." Yet, Ford wisely reasoned that the nation was better off with a dose of laughter, even if it came at his expense.

In 1987 Ford dug deeper, publishing a book titled "Humor and the Presidency," in which he writes, "For those people who wanted to see me in less than 'grand and presidential' circumstances, Chevy Chase and 'Saturday Night Live' provided them with plenty of grist for their mills."

Ford concludes, "The portrayal of me as an oafish ex-jock made for good copy. It was also funny. Maybe not to me, but as much as I might have disliked it, some people were laughing. At the very least, even if no one else was going to laugh, you can be sure the Democrats would!"

6 / I've looked on a lot of women with lust

America's decision to put Jimmy Carter in the White House was a game changer for the Comedy-Industrial Complex. After stressful years with Lyndon Johnson, and deeply dark hours with Richard Nixon, plus the brief, humorless time with Gerald Ford, here was a chief executive with a smile so wide that famed political cartoonist Herbert Block ("Herblock") drew him as the Cheshire Cat from Alice in Wonderland, with a toothy grin that filled the artboard. Winner of three Pulitzer prizes, Herblock wrote in the *Washington Post*, "Many presidents seem to benefit from the public's unhappiness with a predecessor. The disclosures of Nixon's shady operations made Jimmy Carter—a Sunday school teacher who promised always to level with the American people—an acceptable choice." Indeed, voters knew so little about Carter that the slogan "Jimmy Who?" was a favorite among his opponents in both parties. What the nation learned, beyond the fact that Carter had been a Democratic governor of Georgia, was that he ran a peanut farm, had a Southern drawl and famously said in a *Playboy* interview just before the '76 election: "I've looked on a lot of women with lust. I've committed adultery in my heart many times." Seems amazing that

Carter managed to win the election—but it's no surprise that impressionists and comics were overjoyed.

◆ ◆ ◆

CHEVY CHASE STAYED AROUND for the start of SNL's second season, just long enough to help pioneer what would become a staple in presidential parodies: fake debates. With Chase as Ford and Dan Aykroyd as Carter, SNL crafted three debates, the first of which was broadcast on September 18, five days before the real-life candidates held their first debate. In some ways, it was difficult to decide which event was funnier. Roughly 80 minutes into the real debate, Carter was speaking about "a breakdown in trust among our people..." when the audio system went dead. Carter's lips continued to move for another few minutes, but the feed from the 167-year-old Walnut Street Theater in Philadelphia was mute. TV anchor Harry Reasoner jumped in from New York to assure viewers, "This is not a conspiracy against Governor Carter or President Ford." As the snafu continued, Reasoner noted, "We are at the same disadvantage as you. I don't know what they're saying ... Philadelphia may have been isolated from the world for a few minutes. (Pause) Some people think Philadelphia has been isolated from the world for a long time." (Technicians are heard laughing off-camera.) As the delay reached the 27-minute mark, Reasoner quipped, "If you are sort of anti-technology and wish you were back in the 18th century, it's a great night."

In SNL's first debate, Aykroyd went all-in, doing Carter with a wig and reasonably convincing Southern accent, though he insisted on retaining his mustache—perhaps as a way to preserve a bit of his own identity. He told the *Washington Post,* "I don't want to be 'just the guy who did Carter' when I go looking for another job. I remember what happened to Vaughn Meader when Kennedy died."

Chase, meanwhile, played Ford as he had in season one, without trying to look or sound like him...

REPORTER (Jane Curtin): *Mr. President, Governor Carter has accused you of hiding in the White House instead of going out and meeting the people. How do you answer this charge?*

CHASE: *Miss Montgomery, this is of course a ridiculous misnomer. I of course was not hiding. I was simply lost for a bit, and the Secret Service recovered me and I feel just fine.*

SECOND REPORTER (John Belushi): *Governor Carter, your son Chip has admitted to smoking marijuana. What is your attitude on the decriminalization of marijuana?*

AYKROYD: *Mr. Beck, as much as I love my son Chip, if I were to come upon him smoking marijuana I would have to have him arrested. I would, however, grant him an executive pardon but not until he had gone through the due process of the law so all the questions could be answered for the American people. Now, this would be a pardon, not an amnesty. An amnesty would be condoning the smoking of marijuana, whereas this would just be forgiving him for the use of it.*

MODERATOR (Lily Tomlin): *Mr. President, rebuttal?*

CHASE: *Oh, no thank you. I just had dinner.*

Chase debates Aykroyd on SNL.

It was clear that SNL was targeting many of the statements and perceptions that marked the real campaign, such as Carter's effort to remind voters whenever possible that Ford had pardoned Nixon. SNL's next debate came on October 16, ten days after the second real debate. "Chevy did a couple of things that were really brilliant," writer Alan Zweibel told me. "He was playing dim, if you know what I mean. For that second debate, Ford had just been inoculated for swine flu and Chevy appeared with the fucking needle in his arm, right through the suit." Indeed, the syringe remained there for the entire debate—the conceit being that no one in the sketch ever mentioned it. Meanwhile, the focus was on making both candidates appear foolish...

REPORTER (John Belushi): *Mr. Carter, You've been criticized by President Ford for making unfairly bitter personal attacks on him. How do you answer this charge sir?*
AYKROYD: *Bitter? Ah, Mr. Crouse, in the 1930s in Europe,*

a man criticized his personal opponents for their bitter personal attacks on him. And that man was Adolf Hitler. Now, Adolf Hitler was responsible for the deaths of over 50 million people during World War II. Now, I don't believe that Mr. Ford would purposely kill 50 million people, but his lack of leadership may lead to a total, fiery, demonic holocaust.

MODERATOR (Karen Black): *President Ford, rebuttal.*

CHASE: *Well, once again Mr. Carter is playing fast and loose with his figures. During World War II, of course, only 40 million people were killed.*

For SNL's third and final debate, televised just three days before the real election, things got zanier. The moderator, played by Buck Henry, explained that the topics would be "beauty, talent and poise." With that, Aykroyd walked out wearing a 1930s-style swimsuit with a "Mr. Georgia" sash, as Henry announced, "He enjoys catching fish, cleaning and scaling fish, and secretly lusting after fish." Chase, dressed similarly but with flippers on his feet, was introduced by Henry, "He enjoys swimming, football and, inexplicably, sending men into Cambodia." For the "talent" portion, Aykroyd performed dental work on a Secret Service agent, while Chase chose to demonstrate how to use a voting booth—which he knocked over, sending both Chase and the booth tumbling.

◆ ◆ ◆

JIMMY CARTER DEFEATED GERALD FORD by about 1.7 million votes. Dan Aykroyd spent Election Day in Georgia and found the state to be "filled with people who can do Carter."

(Having been born in Ottawa, Canada, it's possible that to him all Georgians sounded alike.) For Carter's inauguration, both Aykroyd and Chase agreed to perform at the formal gala, with Aykroyd playing the President-Elect and Chase portraying Chief Justice Warren Burger, administering the oath of office...

BURGER (Chase): *I will serve all of the people.*

CARTER (Aykroyd): *I will serve all of the people.*

BURGER: *And will serve them*

CARTER: *And will serve them*

BURGER: *Only beer and wine. ...*

BURGER: *My White House shall be a place where all men can drop in for a few cool, frothy beers with my brother Billy. ...*

BURGER: *I promise to be a lusty president.*

CARTER: *I can't say that.*

BURGER: *Just checking to see if you were concentrating. In my heart I do wear women's clothing. Just kidding again, Mr. President. ...*

CARTER: *I'd like to take this opportunity now to say a word about the wonderful set of inauguration coins and medallions on sale in the lobby.*

During the skit, Carter, wife Rosalynn and daughter Amy were laughing heartily. The piece ended with Aykroyd and Chase dancing off stage.

Carter's single term was significant in Aykroyd's career, but there wasn't a lot of competition for the role among impressionists. One Georgian who did develop a convincing Carter imitation was Hans Petersen, a radio host in Augusta. From the moment Carter ran in the New Hampshire primary, almost two years before the general election, Petersen entertained listeners with audio sketches that were similar, in a way, to Vaughn Meader's "The First Family" material.

It had been 15 years since Meader's album captivated the nation, signaling that it was acceptable to laugh at a president and his family. As Bob Booker learned in creating the JFK parody, a gentle approach worked best; rough stuff was better suited to clubs and latenight television. For albums, which might be played over and over in people's homes, a playful touch was desirable. The Carters had many of the same comedic ingredients as the Kennedys. Substitute southern accents for New England twangs...exchange brother Billy (a character in his own right) for Teddy...swap Rosalynn for Jackie...Miss Lillian for Rose Fitzgerald Kennedy...daughter Amy for Caroline...and call "home" a peanut farm rather than the posh environs of Hyannis Port. Plus, trade one leading man with a poofy hairstyle and toothy smile for another, and we see why voters went for Carter and why Hans Petersen decided to make a record album in March, 1977 called "Trust Me."

> CARTER: *Rosalynn, do you know where I left my Levi jacket?*
> ROSALYNN: *I believe you left it downstairs in the Denim Room.*
> CARTER: *No, Sugar, not that one. That's the one with the pearl buttons that I wore last night at the formal state dinner.*
> ROSALYNN: *You mean supper.*

CARTER: *No. Now Puddin', let's go over this again. This is one compromise we have got to make to appease these Yankees up here. A midday meal is lunch, and an evening meal is dinner.*

Petersen's material, like Meader's, was kind-hearted, not likely to distress Democrats or rouse Republicans. Unlike "The First Family," however, "Trust Me" didn't sell 7.5 million copies—although, to be fair, no comedy album has ever equaled that success.

Another quirky record album called "Hail to the Teeth" was released by five Harris brothers. Bert Harris provided the Carter voice, while Bob, Jim, J.T. and Bill played other characters in the sketches. Bill went on to become a Nebraska state senator and also served as mayor of Lincoln. The brothers' 1977 album

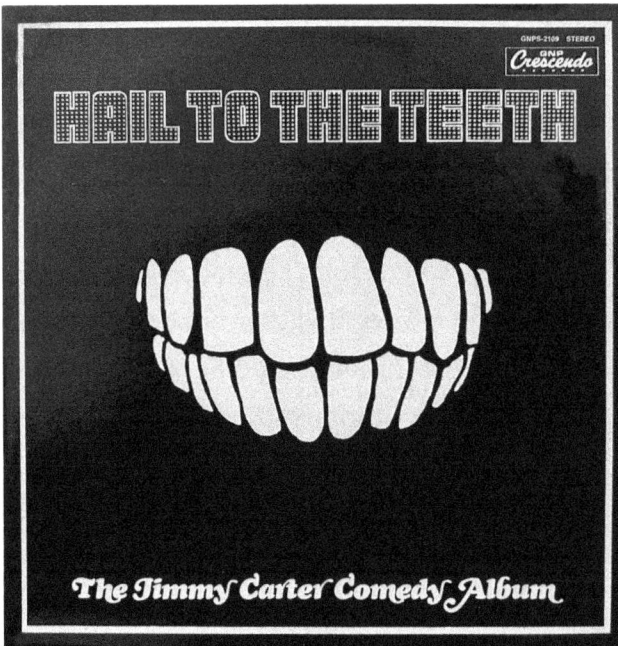

relied in part on the tried-and-true press conference format...

REPORTER: *Do you have any new ideas for alternative sources of energy?*

BERT HARRIS: *As a matter of fact I do. I think that we have completely overlooked the peanut as a potential source of energy.*

REPORTER: *The peanut?*

HARRIS: *That's right. Nothing gives us gas like peanuts.*

REPORTER: *Mister President, it was a long campaign. You had a lot of opponents. You've been in office for several months. Of all the people along the way, who worried you most?*

HARRIS: *I guess I'd have to say, my brother Billy.*

I caught up with Bert at his home, about 60 miles from Plains, Georgia—though back when he recorded the album, at age 26, he and his brothers lived in Nebraska, where Bill served for a while as Jimmy Carter's state campaign chief. "When I was a boy, I heard Vaughn Meader's 'First Family Album' and I was fascinated with that," Harris explains. "It was one of my first impressions, trying to impersonate John Kennedy. We had a friend with a recording studio and we decided to produce an album." That led to several other opportunities, including weekly phone-in spots on more than two dozen radio stations in which Harris would pretend to be the president. Then...

"We were talking about how to get some visibility and one of my brothers says, 'You gotta go on 'Candid Camera.' We had fooled people before. So we went to the lobby of the Red Lion Hotel in downtown Omaha and there was a pay phone. Bob

Rich Little and his Jimmy Carter teeth.

looked up the number for 'Candid Camera' headquarters in New York and I called. A secretary answered, and I said, 'This is Jimmy Carter. I've been a fan of the 'Candid Camera' show all my life. I thought it might be funny to have people reacting to speaking to the president. I wonder if I might speak to Mr. Funt about that.' So she put him on and I said, 'This is not Jimmy Carter, but your secretary thinks I am.' That did it."

Harris to flew to New York where my father had him phone unsuspecting agency workers, pretending to be Carter—with the payoff, "Smile! You're on 'Candid Camera.'"

◆ ◆ ◆

GRADUALLY, TOP COMICS began recovering from the Ford lull and developed Carter impersonations. Rich Little, who has the distinction of performing imitations of every president from Kennedy to Biden, said he perfected his Carter voice by studying the presidential debates. A few days before Carter's inauguration, Little appeared on "The Tonight Show." With his head cocked and flashing a sweeping grin, he declared:

I'm going to keep my promises to the American people, especially to the young people of America. I think the only way to solve the marijuana problem in America today is with a joint session.

Some months later, Little had a set of Chiclets-size upper teeth made, which he carried in his pocket and popped into his mouth whenever he wanted to do Carter. Even Johnny Carson, who had never bothered doing presidential impressions himself on "Tonight," began imitating Carter—with full hair and makeup—in sketches by The Mighty Carson Art Players. But the center of activity remained Studio 8H, where Dan Aykroyd was honing his Carter impression—finally consenting to dye his mustache blond, though still refusing to shave it.

The tasks of writing and rehearsing all week, and then doing 90 minutes of live comedy on Saturday night, was taking a toll on Aykroyd. In their book about SNL, Doug Hill and Jeff Weingrad report: "Danny was working so hard and was so tightly wound in the first place that his frustrations increasingly erupted into violence. Fist through the walls of his office and dressing room were the least of it. He once came offstage unhappy about the way a sketch had gone and smashed his hand through the glass covering a poster outside the studio, cutting himself fairly deeply in the process. Another time he smashed a glassed-in directory by the elevator on 17 and left a trail of blood on his way to the NBC infirmary on the seventh floor."

Less than a year into the Carter Administration, SNL was sharpening its barbs. Ray Charles, a musical guest in Season 3, explained that he grew up in a small town near Plains,

Georgia, so, "I have a special warm feeling for our president. It's not because we're neighbors, but you see, at one time his family owned my grandfather. So, therefore, Jimmy, this is for you." He proceeds to sing his classic hit "Georgia," as the scene shifts to the Oval Office...

> CARTER (Aykroyd): *Good evening. Throughout my campaign I spoke of the intelligence of the American people. It was with this optimism that I introduced my energy program. But now my energy program is in severe trouble, mainly because you, the American public, have failed to understand the urgency of the energy crisis, even though I have explained it to you many times, slowly, clearly and using one-syllable words. Words like oil, gas, oil, gas. I said our economy and national security depended on a comprehensive energy program. But did you respond? No. ... I probably won't get re-elected. Everything's just going down the toilet. ... In 1977, you blew it. Thank you, and goodnight.*

Though years remained in Carter's term, Aykroyd's routine was prescient—not just in predicting another change for the nation in 1980, but in forecasting that Americans would eventually come to realize that Jimmy Carter was a more skilled statesman than impressionists made him out to be.

Meanwhile, new heights were about to be reached for acting presidents when American voters made an actor their president.

7 / Well . . .

*"There have been times in this office when I wondered
how you could do the job if you hadn't been an actor."*
—*Ronald Reagan, as he ended his second term*

The night before Ronald Reagan's inauguration in 1981, he and wife Nancy donned formal attire and sat on high-backed blue velvet chairs among 20,000 invited guests at the Capital Centre in Landover, Maryland, for a celebratory gala produced by Frank Sinatra. In the audience were many show-biz notables including Bob Hope and Dean Martin. The master of ceremonies was Johnny Carson. And the featured performer was Rich Little, whose act that night consisted of impersonating Nixon, Ford, Carter and—most impressively—Reagan.

The real-life president-in-waiting practically convulsed with laughter on his velvet cushion as "Ford" was asked, "What are your thoughts on Jimmy Carter becoming president?" The answer: "I think that Jimmy Carter as president is like Truman Capote marrying Dolly Parton. The job was just too big for him to handle."

As the evening progressed it was increasingly clear that

Reagan and his conservative Hollywood cronies were keen on making the most of this new opportunity in Washington, D.C.—almost the way the "Beverly Hillbillies" behaved upon arriving in new digs, except with better jewelry. And Reagan was eager to laugh as Little portrayed him...

QUESTION: *You have said that you are going to raise defense spending, cut taxes, balance the budget, all at the same time. How do you propose to do this?*

REAGAN (Little): *Well, it's very, very simple. I'm going to keep two sets of books.*

... QUESTION: *Do you have any animosity toward President Carter?*

REAGAN: *No. You know, I didn't mind when Jimmy left me inflation, when he left me unemployment, when he left me a recession. But I sure hope he's coming back for Billy and Miss Lillian. They're still sitting in the Oval Office saying, "What the hell happened?"*

Reagan celebrates with pal Rich Little.

By 1981, Reagan had already served multiple terms as president—of the Screen Actors Guild. He appeared in 53 mediocre films before turning to politics, becoming governor of California in 1966 and serving for eight years. In '76 he lost his bid for the GOP presidential nomination but captured the spot in 1980 and then won 44 states in a landslide victory over Carter. Though he considered himself a Democrat during his acting days, Reagan became a Republican and a beacon of conservatism. His inaugural speech was marked by the memorable assertion, "Government is not the solution to our problem, government is the problem." Reagan reduced taxes for the wealthy, cut back government regulations and increased military spending. Some of his speeches were peppered with dog-whistle phrases designed to appeal to racists. But he managed to usher in a period of prosperity for many Americans, and with that became one of the nation's most admired, and widely impersonated, U.S. presidents.

Veteran political reporter and Reagan biographer Lou Cannon wrote in the *Washington Post*, "Few politicians understood the distinction between seriousness of purpose and taking oneself too seriously as well as Reagan, who relentlessly poked fun at himself and his fellow conservatives. Asked after his election in 1966 what kind of governor he would be, Reagan replied, 'I don't know, I've never played a governor.' At a Gridiron Club dinner early in his presidency, Reagan quipped, 'Sometimes in our administration the right hand doesn't know what the far right hand is doing.'"

♦ ♦ ♦

RICH LITTLE WAS ARGUABLY the nation's most skilled impersonator in the '70s and '80s—a frequent guest on prime-time variety shows and a semi-regular on "The Tonight Show." He imitated Hollywood denizens such as John Wayne, Jimmy Stewart, George Burns and Jack Benny, while befriending many of them, particularly the more politically conservative. He also focused on politicians, developing an act in which he imitated multiple presidents doing faux interviews with legendary CBS anchorman Walter Cronkite, who Little also portrayed.

Born in 1938, Little grew up in Ottawa, Canada, the son of a urologist father and a stay-at-home mom. Spending most weekends at local movie houses, he studied screen stars of the period and became adept at mimicking their voices. At 17, Little and his friend Geoff Scott created an act with their impersonations, winning a talent competition on CBOT in Ottawa. That led to an appearance on "Pick the Stars," a national contest broadcast by the CBC, and another first prize.

Little had just turned 24, working in radio and local theater in Canada, when Vaughn Meader's "The First Family" was released in the U.S. Little and his radio partner, Les Lye, created a derivative album called "My Fellow Canadians," which had sketches similar to the Kennedy spoofs—except the characters were all Canadian, starting with Prime Minister John Diefenbaker. Released by Capitol Records' Canadian division, the album was surprisingly successful. However, Little also had the misfortune to create a Christmas album in Canada just before the Kennedy assassination in which he portrays JFK as the Spirit of Christmas Present, uttering the regrettable line, "Scrooge, my life upon the globe is brief; it ends tonight. In fact, it ends as fast as you can say your name." The album was withdrawn from stores immediately after Kennedy's death.

But Little's star was rising. Canada's biggest magazine, *Maclean's*, called him, "the world's most successful mimic, grossing about $100,000 a year, conjuring from a card-index memory 126 dead-on impressions of the famous." He got his big break in the U.S. on the CBS variety program hosted by Judy Garland, and quickly became a frequent guest across the American TV dial.

I spoke with Little in 2022 as he neared his 84th birthday, still doing shows in Las Vegas and appearing frequently on Trinity, the Christian cable network. "My audience is mostly conservative," he explains rather proudly. "I'd say about 90 percent." Little's personal views haven't changed much over time, but Vegas crowds—just like cable-TV audiences—are more sharply divided than ever. "There are a few people in my audience, not many, who are real lefties. They're Democratic supporters, and they don't like my Biden at all. They just don't want anybody to make fun of Biden no matter what. They get a little disgruntled."

I've watched more hours of tape on Rich Little than most NFL coaches devote to Sunday's opponent. Though I find his personal politics off-putting, there's no question that he is among the best performers doing POTUS impressions. He's portrayed all 12 presidents since Kennedy and met eight of them, in a career spanning six decades. I asked him for his takes on the first five presidents he mastered.

Kennedy: "He had a very distinctive voice, but that (Boston) accent was difficult to do. If you didn't get the accent, you wouldn't have Kennedy." Little says that back in the sixties he got better reactions imitating Vaughn Meader than imitating JFK. "I think Meader exaggerated it more. Accentuated the accent a little more. The real JFK wasn't as exciting as what Vaughn Meader did."

Johnson: "He had that Southern drawl and put his glasses down at the end of his nose, and he lowered his voice when he said things like, 'My fellow Americans...'"

Nixon: "His mannerisms are very important. You've got to get the body language. Nixon always wore the same blue suit, and he never took the hanger out of it, so he was very stiff."

Ford: "He had sort of a monotone voice; not very exciting. But he was a great, great guy. I had a podium made that looked like wood but it was made out of cork, so when I did my Ford I would stumble and fall on the podium and it would break in half. One time down in Palm Springs. I was doing a benefit for the Betty Ford Clinic. Frank Sinatra and Gerald Ford were sitting below me on a very high stage. And when I hit the podium, instead of breaking in half it smashed and a million pieces of cork flew into the air. I grabbed the microphone and fell off the stage and landed in Gerald Ford's lap. When I realized I hadn't killed him, I put the microphone up to his lips and he went, 'Whoops.' And Frank Sinatra was on the floor, pounding the floor, with tears streaming down his face, he was laughing so hard."

Reagan: "Well, you've got to say 'well,' and the body language is very important because he always walked with his hand stretched out and the head bobbing." (Little once asked Reagan, "Mr. President, why is it that you always look down before you speak?" Reagan replied, "Well, Rich, you'd look down, too, if you owned a horse ranch.") "He had a very distinctive voice that always got a great reaction. I used to do memory jokes on him

Little pranks Reagan by replacing the presidential seal with one that reads "In Rich We Trust," as Nancy Reagan looks on.

because, you know, his memory loss (from Alzheimer's disease) eventually killed him. But even back in the days he was president I would do some memory jokes and he would laugh. He loved them. He wasn't sensitive at all."

Little admired and befriended Reagan. In his memoir, "Little by Little," he writes: "The first time I met him he was giving a press conference at the White House. He said, 'Rich, I'm glad you're here. You do me better than I do, so you finish this damn press conference. I'm going for a sandwich.' That was my introduction to Reagan. And then he turned to me and said, 'Just don't get me into a war.'"

♦ ♦ ♦

JOHNNY CARSON RARELY DID political impersonations, yet he made Reagan a recurring character on "The Tonight Show," using full makeup and wig. Unlike Rich Little, who befriended

Republican politicians, Carson was no fan of Reagan's policies—though he was determined to keep viewers in the dark about his personal views. "He was trying to be an entertainer and not to be a political pundit," Carson's nephew, Jeff Sotzing, told me. Sotzig worked as a producer for his uncle and today serves as president of Carson Entertainment. "There was a time when he was making jokes about Nixon and Watergate," he recalls. "And it came back to him that Nixon was disturbed about it—he was drinking in the middle of the night and watching the show. And at that point, [Johnny] said, 'You know what, we're not going to do this anymore. We're not going to be cruel. We're trying to be humorous. We're trying to be entertaining, and you don't need to make any political statements.' Besides, why alienate half the audience?"

By the time Reagan took office Carson had been doing "The Tonight Show" for almost two decades, so perhaps his concerns about alienating viewers had receded. Carson had the voice to do a good Reagan, and with the proper hairpiece and makeup was actually able to pass for the president, as happened at an NBC affiliates gathering at the Century Plaza Hotel, where Carson took the stage as Reagan and for a while had many in the audience completely fooled. This was a time when Reagan was known as the "Teflon President" because criticism—and comedic parodies—never seemed to stick to him. His job approval, though higher than the three presidents who preceded him, was not exceptional. To his good fortune, however, his popularity remained high, even as his performance in office sagged.

The thread connecting Reagan and Carson was Fred de Cordova, the Emmy-winning producer who worked on "The

Tonight Show" for 22 years. Early in his career he directed "Bedtime for Bonzo," a quirky film about a chimpanzee whose trainer tries to teach him human morals, described by *Variety* as "a lot of beguiling nonsense with enough broad situations to gloss over plot holes." The chimp's trainer was played by Reagan.

"Freddie and Reagan were very close," says Sotzing. "It was a running joke that when Reagan came into town for an event, Freddie got an invitation and Johnny didn't."

A year into Reagan's presidency, Carson did a routine that his nephew describes as "probably Johnny's favorite sketch of all time. They did it live, and they knocked it out of the park." Based on Abbott & Costello's "Who's on First?" gag, it featured actor Fred Holliday as White House Chief of Staff James Baker and Carson as Reagan, meeting in the Oval Office just before a press conference...

> REAGAN: *Well, now, the environment's on their minds and, well, I'm sure they'll ask me about my secretary of the interior.*
> BAKER: *Watt.*
> REAGAN: *I said I'm sure they'll ask me about my secretary of the interior.*
> BAKER: *Watt.*
> REAGAN: *Jim, I just told you, I think they'll ask about my secretary of the interior.*
> BAKER: *James Watt. You're scheduled to go swimming with him tomorrow morning at the Y.*
> REAGAN: *Where?*
> BAKER: *Y.*
> REAGAN: *Why?*

BAKER: *That's right. With Watt.*

REAGAN: *With what? I don't even know with who, Jim.*

BAKER: *Not who, Watt.*

REAGAN: *Well, now, let's get this straight. I'm going swimming tomorrow with who?*

BAKER: *Watt.*

REAGAN: *Where?*

BAKER: *Y.*

And so it went for four minutes, with the conversation shifting to other names that confused Reagan, such as "Hu" (the Chinese leader). A few years later Carson would do his other Reagan favorite, reciting a holiday classic...

Well, 'twas the night before Christmas when all through the White House, Not a creature was stirring, not even my spouse;

The stockings were hung by the chimney with care, And my tax bill in Congress had not a prayer.

With full makeup, Johnny Carson does his Reagan on "The Tonight Show."

♦ ♦ ♦

WITH REAGAN'S POPULARITY, plus the expansion of media outlets in the early '80s through explosive development of cable-TV channels, demand for Reagan routines was growing exponentially. Rich Little teamed with one of Vaughn Meader's original producers to create a record album called "The First Family Rides Again." (Reporter: "What would you like to be doing after you leave office?" Reagan: "Breathing.") Spoofs about Reagan became so prevalent that one even made it to off-Broadway: a satiric musical review titled "Rap Master Ronnie," co-written by "Doonesbury" cartoonist Garry Trudeau. The production featured 16 original songs—although only one truly qualified as rap—each lampooning an aspect of Reagan's programs and character. "If you're right 90 percent of the time, why quibble over the remaining 3 percent?" crooned Reathel Bean as Reagan, who at the time was running for a second term.

"I don't know if there's anything artistic being done about this election—it is either being ignored or given up on," Trudeau told my colleague at the time, Stephen Holden of *The New York Times*. "It didn't seem right to me to let it go without trying to say something. The piece is enormously challenging because, as everybody knows, Reagan has proven unusually resistant to frontal assault. That's a very difficult target to take aim at."

The show ran for a year in New York and then opened in Los Angeles with John Roarke as Reagan. It was later revived on pay-cable by Cinemax, starring impressionist Jim Morris.

"Saturday Night Live," meanwhile, which should have

John Roarke as Reagan, whom he played on "Fridays" as well as in the Los Angeles cast of Garry Trudeau's "Rap Master Ronnie."

been leading the Reagan surge, was struggling. After five ground-breaking but exhausting seasons, Lorne Michaels wanted time off, or at least some relief from hands-on producing. When talks between Michaels and NBC broke down, he left for what would turn out to be five years in exile. The new showrunner, Jean Doumanian, who had been SNL's associate producer, was faced with not only filling Michaels' shoes but also replacing the cast and writing staff. Some left because their five-year deals were up, while others simply followed Michaels as he left his office, which Doumanian reportedly spent $22,000 redecorating.

The first show of SNL's sixth season—delayed until November 15 of 1980 because of production problems—was a mess. The cold open featured the new cast's brightest performer, Joe Piscopo, playing outgoing President Carter in the Oval Office. Piscopo is a competent impersonator, but the material he worked with that night was awful—"Carter" blaming Jews for his election loss. ("Those beanyheads didn't vote for me.") At the end of the sketch, Carter says he can now do what he's wanted to do for four years and proceeds to take a revolver to the Rose Garden to kill his brother Billy. Marvin Kitman of *Newsday* said the new edition should have been called "Saturday Night Dead on Arrival."

The most egregiously miscast newcomer was Charles Rocket, who introduced himself to viewers as "kind of a cross between Chevy Chase and Bill Murray." Though tall and vaguely similar in appearance to Chase, Rocket was more of a cross between a slightly funny telephone pole and a completely unfunny telephone pole. Doumanian gave him the plum "Weekend Update" anchor role as well as the task of impersonating the new president. Soon after Reagan took office Rocket appeared in a humorless sketch in which Amy Carter is left behind at the White House to live with the Reagans, with Amy explaining to the president (Rocket), "I want to wear makeup just like you."

One of the replacement writers, Barry Blaustein, who went on to do the screenplay for Eddie Murphy's film "Coming to America," said the new staff quickly realized "the whole world unanimously hated you." I pointed out to Blaustein that SNL tried Rocket, Piscopo, Harry Shearer, Randy Quaid and even Robin Williams as Ronald Reagan and nothing clicked. "I don't recall any sketches we did with Reagan that were memorable," he conceded. "I hate to say that."

In fact, there were some memorable Reagan routines being done at that time—across the dial on ABC's derivative series "Fridays." The show never generated much attention and lasted only three seasons, but it featured a talented cast including

Larry David, Michael Richards (Kramer on "Seinfeld") and John Roarke, who played a convincing Reagan, with Melanie Chartoff as his wife Nancy. "Fridays" delivered daring political sketches that were reminiscent of "That Was the Week That Was" and counter-culture improv groups like The Committee, managing to combine funny impressions with powerful political statements. ("Fridays" shared a studio in LA with "The Lawrence Welk Show," creating under one roof what might have been the most culturally severe juxtaposition in TV history.)

Now retired and living in Rhode Island, John Roarke took me through his memory book. "I was in the fifth grade, when Vaughn Meader's album, 'The First Family' came out. I didn't know anything about politics, but we had that comedy album, and I came home after school and played it every day for about a year. To me it was like going to church. I was just taken with the idea of somebody imitating the president and getting huge laughs. Years later I became the first guy to do Reagan on television."

Roarke says it took him a while to perfect his Reagan, but what finally clicked were traits he copied from his grandmother's best friend, a woman named Ada McHugh. "She had this way of looking befuddled and I took that and made it one of Reagan's mannerisms. I found a way to walk with my hips locked while the top of my body would sway from one side to the other—and it was McHugh.

"Reagan would wobble his head once in a while. I exaggerated the wobble and finally I'd get distracted from what I was saying, by the wobbling, and I'd take my two hands and slap both sides of my head in order to stop the wobbling, which became a very funny gag."

One weekend late in 1980 provided a vivid example of what "Fridays" had managed to accomplish with presidential parodies, and how far SNL's efforts at political humor had fallen. Let's first examine SNL's cold open on December 13, running all of 90 seconds, with three cast members standing in front of a curtain. There was no scenery, costumes or props. Here is the complete transcript:

> DENNY DILLON: *Hello, we're speaking to you on behalf of an organization of decent moral Americans.*
> GAIL MATTHIUS: *We're the folks who listened to the preachers on television who told us to vote conservative. We did and we won. So listen up losers.*
> CHARLES ROCKET: *So, who are we?*
> DILLON: *We're the Mean Majority. We're very, very mean.*
> MATTHIUS: *Who are we mean to? Just about everybody.*
> ROCKET: *We believe that the vast majority of Americans in their hearts are like us, mean. And these last 20 years of civil rights was just an attempt to be nice.*
> MATTHIUS: *Those days are over.*
> DILLION: *And You-Know-Who told us so. He's like us: mean!*
> ROCKET: *He told us to tell you, the television viewers of America, that there are certain TV shows you are not to watch so you better not. The shows are...*
> DILLON: *"Sex in a Condo."*
> ROCKET: *"Wet Tee-Shirt Party."*

MATTHIUS: *"Let's Spit on the Flag."*
DILLON: *And there's another one. I can't remember the name. It's, Live...*
ROCKET: *...From New York...*
MATTHIUS: *...It's...*
DILLON: *...Saturday Night!*

The audience in Studio 8H barely chuckled, but one imagines writers and performers at ABC were cracking up, considering what they had pulled off on "Fridays" 24 hours earlier: An 18-minute, fully-produced opening parody titled, "The Ronny Horror Picture Show." With elaborate sets and costumes, plus original song and dance, the sketch was a marvel of live television and a brilliant dissection of Reagan and his new era of conservative politics. Like the film, "The Rocky Horror Picture Show," released in theaters five years earlier and based on a stage production that preceded it, the "Ronny" version begins with a close-up of disembodied bright red lips, telling voters they got what they deserved...

Politicians, double dealers;
Special interests, faithless healers.
See young men fighting, worker layoffs;
Slush fund scandals, corporate payoffs.
Whoa, ho, ho, ho...
It's the eighties, Ronny Reagan Horror Show.

On a stormy night, two young liberal activists take refuge at an eerie mansion. They encounter a band of evil conservatives who explain in song, "Let's Fight the Big One Again" (a parody of "Time Warp")...

It's been a nation, under sedation,
Where liberals have run the show.
But things are changing, maybe not for the better,
We—have seized control.
... It's good for the wealthy,
Who can afford to stay healthy.
And the underprivileged,
You won't see at all.
Just a bit of a tax cut,
And the end of a gun butt,
And everyone opposed to us will fall.

Enter John Roarke as Reagan (Tim Curry's Dr. Frank-N-Furter), the mad scientist, who does a masterful send-up of "Sweet Transvestite," with Reagan in fishnets and heels.

I'm an arch-conservative, anti-intellectual, chief
executive, From Californ-i-hahaha!

Everything changes when Reagan's lab-created monster turns out to be a Black Panther, who leads the cast in "Let's Fight the System," and the sketch ends with fists raised as Reagan is vanquished.

The studio audience stood and applauded—a rarity in Hollywood productions. "What we tried to do with the political satire," Roarke explains, "is make a sharp comment upon what was happening in politics in sort of a deep message kind of way while being funny about it."

Would you say all you guys on "Fridays" were progressives?

"Yes, yes. And the director of the show, Jack Burns of

Burns and Schreiber fame, he was very left, a very liberal guy. In fact he worked for Bobby Kennedy at one point."

Were you cognisant of what SNL was doing each week?

"No. I think the higher up you went on the food chain, the producers, they were. But the cast and the writers, we really did our own thing."

The material on "Fridays" was uneven at times, but the show was gaining in popularity until the news program "Night-line" was given an extra night on ABC's schedule, pushing "Fridays" to a later start time—and soon thereafter to cancellation.

◆ ◆ ◆

BACK AT NBC, Jean Doumanian was fired after 10 disastrous months and replaced by Dick Ebersol, who was not keen on political sketches but did manage to boost the show's humor quotient by hiring Eddie Murphy, Billy Crystal and Martin Short. By the time Ebersol stepped aside in 1985, with Lorne Michaels returning, the show was in danger of being canceled. Michaels revamped the cast yet again, with breakout performers Dana Carvey and Phil Hartman. Toward the end of Reagan's second term, Hartman, one of SNL's most versatile impressionists, made his first appearance as Reagan in a piece titled "Mastermind." The sketch played on Reagan's reputation as a slow-witted nice guy in public, but imagined that in private he might actually be a shrewd manipulator. He's seen, for instance, posing for a PR photo with a Girl Scout, doddering and barely able to stay awake; as soon as the press leaves, he snaps into action and gives his staff a dizzying set of complex directives without a trace of enfeeblement. It was funny, and Hartman was superb.

The sketch was written by Robert Smigel, one of the more gifted contributors at SNL. He recounted for me how the show's Reagan material had become stale and predictable. "Mastermind," he said, "was almost as much about comedy as it was about politics. That's why it was so funny to people because they had only seen this other version of Reagan portrayed, not only in comedy, but just in general. We played on the absurdity that Reagan not only knows everything about Iran Contra, but that he's running the whole thing."

We'll hear more from Smigel, who played a major role in crafting the impressions of several presidents. But before leaving Reagan, a word from John Roarke of "Fridays" about the challenges impressionists face as they immerse themselves in their roles. We reflected on the sad way in which his inspiration, Vaughn Meader, as well as his idol, David Frye, ended their careers in spirals of despair. Roarke, who studied Reagan intensely, offered this:

"If you get into the character, you can kind of forget who you are sometimes. And if you do a lot of characters, and if you do it like I did, which is you really tried to not copy them but get into their heads and get into their souls, then you've got to watch it so you don't lose yourself. Not that you're going to become psychotic, but it's unsettling when you spend more time being other people than being yourself."

8 / *Na ga da it*

A l Franken was in a small chartered plane, traveling from
Boston to New York on a clear November night in 1988.
Gazing at the lights below, his thoughts turned to "the
majesty of democracy"—despite the fact that he and other supporters of Democrat Michael Dukakis suffered a resounding
defeat in the presidential election earlier that day. Franken and

fellow SNL cast member Jon Lovitz had gone to Boston at the invitation of the Dukakis campaign to entertain at what was supposed to be a victory party, with Franken as emcee and Lovitz doing his finely honed Dukakis impersonation. As they took the stage, the mood was already grim. By the time they boarded the plane to go home, George H.W. Bush had declared victory at a ballroom in Houston, standing in front of a banner proclaiming, "America Wins." As Franken recalls the flight with Lovitz, "I was a little sad but I'm just thinking like, you know, what a great country we are. I'm looking down at the lights and then Jon says, 'Fuck! Bush is President.' And I went like, 'Well, yeah, but you know that's the way the system works.' And he says, 'Fucking Dana gets to do the president.'"

By selecting Bush over Dukakis, voters had decreed that Carvey, not Lovitz, would be SNL's lead impressionist for at least the next four years, with a starring role in many cold opens.

That night Lovitz phoned Dana Carvey and screamed into the phone, "You won!"

♦ ♦ ♦

ALTHOUGH BUSH HAD SERVED eight years as Reagan's vice president, he was rarely impersonated, which was just as well since Bush's delivery was dry and his charisma minimal. Besides, with Reagan to spoof there was little reason to give Bush much attention.

At SNL, Lorne Michaels was back from exile with a refurbished staff that featured talented contributors including Carvey, Lovitz and Franken, and the weeks leading up to the '88 election gave SNL its quadrennial opportunity to mock a presidential campaign. Lovitz was an immediate success as Dukakis, managing to both look and sound like the diminutive Massachusetts governor. Dukakis provided plenty of parody points beyond his appearance: He was overly analytical, seemingly uptight and generally humorless. He had an unfortunate habit of awkwardly incorporating foreign language in his speeches—something Lovitz enjoyed mocking. At a campaign stop in Louisville, for example, the real Dukakis criticized White House ethics under President Reagan by using a Greek phrase that translated as a "fish rots from the head down." Perhaps the biggest blunder in the '88 campaign came when Dukakis was photographed riding in an M-1A1 battle tank wearing a high-tech helmet that aides warned would look silly. Worse than silly, it became the centerpiece of Bush's attack ads.

As for Vice President Bush, he offered little in the way of hooks for impressionists. "Dana had nothing," recalls Franken. "If you listen to his first few attempts, Dana just didn't have that handle. And we're going, 'Oh, boy, Bush is just kind of boring.'"

Carvey says it took him a year to nail Bush, having failed rather miserably in one 1987 sketch in which he didn't look like Bush (no glasses) and struggled with the vice president's voice. In an essay Carvey wrote for *The New York Times* on the occasion of Bush's death in 2018, he explained...

"President Ronald Reagan was an easy target. He had an impossibly low hairline, a tan, wrinkled face, a bobbling head, and as a bonus, he called his wife Mommy. He was comedy gold.

"On the other hand, the first President Bush was a comedian's nightmare. There was nothing to do an impression of—no hook. My take on him, in the early sketches, was actually kind of terrible and not particularly funny."

With the help of Franken and veteran SNL writer Jim Downey, he gradually added gestures and phrases that elevated his Bush impression. As with Chevy Chase's Gerald Ford routines, they were exaggerations or, in some notable cases, totally fake.

Franken: "The root of it was Dana and I playing around, him kind of doing the 'not gonna go there' kind of thing, and me laughing. That was part of my contribution. As he says, 'laughter is the oxygen of comedy.'"

Carvey: "At one point, I raised my right arm and began rotating my hand lazily with index finger pointed—as if the hand were reaching for some thought. And then it came out—my voice flattening in a lazy syntax—'those people out there ... doing that thing ... doing that thing in that whole area over there.' Al was laughing his ass off, and we both knew we had a hook. At that moment, President Bush became a character."

Over the four years of Bush's presidency, Carvey added what he calls "sub-hooks," including the relentlessly funny, "Na ga da it" (not going to do it) and, "It wouldn't be prudent at this juncture." For the record: The real George H.W. Bush insisted he never uttered any such things.

◆ ◆ ◆

DANA CARVEY REMEMBERS LISTENING to a 1965 record album distributed by Collier's Encyclopedia called "Year-in-Sound." One track included an interview with the Beatles—and Dana, age 10 at the time, impressed his family by doing an imitation that wasn't so much any particular Beatle but sort of a generic Beatle. "That was the first time I thought I could alter my voice and make people laugh." His parents, both teachers, had moved the family from Missoula, Montana to San Carlos, California, when Dana was three. "By the time I was in fifth grade, when asked, 'What do you want to do with your life?' I wrote, 'Be a comedian and make a hundred thousand a year.'"

Carvey attended junior college in San Mateo and finished at San Francisco State University with a degree in broadcast communications. Working weekends in small clubs, often for no pay, he won the 1977 San Francisco Stand-Up Comedy Competition. "There's a picture of me standing there at 22, having just won that thing, which levitated me to the moon. And behind me is Mort Sahl and Robin Williams, and they gave me the check" ($500, which he used to buy a guitar). A big break came when NBC signed him to a contract that paid $50,000 while the net-

Carvey at 22, winning the San Francisco Stand-Up award.

work figured out something for him to do. He was cast in a 1982 sitcom with Mickey Rooney and Nathen Lane called "One of the Boys"—named by *TV Guide* as one of the worst shows of all time. Several other failed TV projects and a few movie parts followed, all of which paid well but convinced Carvey that stand-up comedy was really his thing.

Cut to Igby's, a small comedy club in West Los Angeles, in the summer of '86. Lorne Michaels and NBC's president Brandon Tartikoff—along with Cher, who happened to be accompanying them that evening—are seated among 180 customers watching Carvey do a 40-minute set. ("Great crowd, not an industry crowd. I played there a lot and killed in the room.") Carvey says he realized this was the culmination of everything he had worked for since high school. ("I'm confident, but I'm terrified.") Two weeks earlier he had done a one-nighter at a pizza parlor in Martinez and four people showed up, "and half of them hated me." At Igby's he did Church Lady and sang "Choppin' Broccoli," his parody about a pretentious rock star: "Everything you say is suddenly terribly important. It doesn't have to make any literal sense." Carvey was 31 at the time, but with shaggy blond hair and a baby face, looked to be about 18. He did well enough to be invited to a formal audition at a TV studio in Burbank, where the competition included Jim Carrey. Carvey got the job, but Carrey was hired a few years later as a regular on the Fox sketch series "In Living Color," where he impersonated George H.W. Bush at the very time that Carvey was killing as Bush on SNL. Clearly, NBC bested Fox on that one.

◆ ◆ ◆

A MONTH BEFORE the '88 election SNL reached the top of its game in a debate sketch featuring Carvey as Bush and Lovitz as Dukakis, with Tom Hanks as ABC's Peter Jennings, Jan Hooks doing a marvelous job portraying moderator Diane Sawyer, and Kevin Nealon in the role of obnoxious questioner Sam Donaldson. The two candidates stepped behind their podiums and Lovitz could barely see over the top of his—until he pushed a button triggering a hydraulic lift that raised him to an imposing height (a sight gag created by SNL writer at the time, Conan O'Brien).

Carvey still hadn't perfected his Bush character, but the writing by Franken and Downey carried the sketch. At one point, Bush is asked about feeding the nation's hungry...

BUSH (Carvey): *That's a big problem. Unfortunately the format of these debates makes it very hard to give a complete answer. If I had more time I could spell out in greater detail, but I'm afraid, unfortunately, in a short-answer session like this all I can say is, we are on the track. We're getting the job done. We can do more. But let's stay the course. A thousand points of light. Well, unfortunately I see my time is up.*

SAWYER (Hooks): *Mr. Vice President, you still have a minute 20.*

BUSH: *Diane, I must have spoken for at least two minutes.*

SAWYER: *No, just 40 seconds Mr. Vice President.*

BUSH: *Really? Well, I must have used up that time just in talking about it right now.*

SAWYER: *No, Mr. Vice President, it's not being counted against you.*

BUSH: *Well, I just wouldn't want to take up some of Governor Dukakis's time.*

SAWYER: *It won't. It will come out of the post debate commentary.*

BUSH: *You think that's a good idea?*

SAWYER: *(Nods) You still have a minute 20, Mr. Vice President.*

BUSH: *Well, sure, more has to be done. But the program is in place. Make no mistake, we are doing the job. So let's just stay the course and keep on track. Stay the course.*

SAWYER: *You still have 50 seconds left, Mr. Vice President.*

BUSH: *Well, let me just sum up. On track. Stay the course. A thousand points of light. Stay the course.*

SAWYER: *Governor Dukakis, rebuttal.*

DUKAKIS (Lovitz): *I can't believe I'm losing to this guy.*

Al Franken wrote the Dukakis line. According to Carvey and Downey it got SNL's biggest laugh of the season. Downey explains, "It was a commentary on Bush, but it was also a commentary on Dukakis's confidence. He was unshakeable and always acted like he had just kicked ass."

Franken, a progressive, and Downey, somewhat right of center, collaborated on much of SNL's best political stuff. "I had the superstar team," says Carvey, "because Jim and Al are different flavors of writer. And having both, and me in the center, the three of us really created this thing. It got huge."

Franken: "We didn't feel it was our job as writers to have a political point of view, you know, whether Republican, conservative or liberal. And it certainly wasn't Lorne's goal to do that. We had, like, seven cast members, we had all these writers, and we just didn't feel it was right. We tried to do the best well-observed comedy and satire that we could do. We tried to reward people for knowing stuff and not punish them for not."

♦ ♦ ♦

A PLUM GIG FOR IMPRESSIONISTS is the annual White House Correspondents' Dinner. Alas, for everyone else the event is no longer the good idea it appeared to be when started a century ago, with attendance by presidents beginning with Calvin Cooledge in 1924. In recent years the gala, described derisively as Nerd Prom, has become an embarrassingly misguided exercise at which media types rub overdressed shoulders with the people they are supposed to cover objectively. It has gradually moved beyond its original mission—of intramural fun and fund-raising among journalists—and toward what Jimmy Kimmel said when he headlined the event in 2012: "Everything that is wrong with America is in this room tonight." Members of the WHCA would be quick to point out that the dinner raises money for scholarships and other worthwhile programs to support journalists. But good intentions notwithstanding, the "roast" format is so outdated that in 2022 President Biden told the crowd, "Tonight we come here to answer a very important question that's on everyone's mind: Why the hell are we doing this?"

For those who play POTUS the dinner has provided a

unique platform, but results have been mixed at best. Chevy Chase did his bumbling Gerald Ford routine in 1976, but the black-tie crowd didn't find it nearly as funny as Chase's similar bits on SNL. In 1984, with Ronald Reagan running for re-election, Rich Little provided the entertainment—which was largely a broadside against Reagan's predecessor, Jimmy Carter, delivered by Little while Reagan sat a few feet away, laughing hysterically. But in 1989 something rather remarkable happened at the WHCD. An impressionist named Jim Morris stepped to the microphone, put on a pair of Bush-style glasses, gestured awkwardly without speaking for 20 painful seconds, and then asked, "How are ya?" What followed was a symphony of non sequiturs, delivered in an amazingly accurate Bush voice.

> We're celebrating the first hundred, whatever, we got there. And I think it's a time that, you know, there's no mel-azze, nothing of the kind. I think this is the time we give thanks for what we have is, well, what have you.

He summed up:

> There's a new breeze blowin' out there, and we're breakin' new wind.

Personal note: I happened to be watching the Correspondents' Dinner that night on C-SPAN. Though Morris was relatively unknown, he was so impressive that I reached out a few days later and booked him for an appearance on "Candid Camera." We shot the gag at a catering company in New Canaan, Connecticut, where temp workers were told to expect calls from "celebrities who would be participating in a charity gala." Soon the calls came, from Ted Koppel, Julia Child, Andy Rooney and

President Bush hams it up with Jim Morris in Washington.

President George H.W. Bush. Of course, the voices were all provided by Morris in the next room. It was a funny sequence, and
one of the rare "Candid Camera" scenes in which the performer
working for us stole the show from the unsuspecting folks we
were secretly photographing.

♦ ♦ ♦

THE MORE YOU LEARN ABOUT IMPRESSIONISTS, the
more you realize that many are bound by common threads. Jim
Morris, who grew up in Framingham, Massachusetts, recounts
nights at the dinner table when he sat across from his uncle
Morty, imitating his distinctive Jewish accent ("Could ya pass
the matzoh balls already.") He says that as a young teen ("my

deformative years") he was able to do three impressions: Truman Capote, Lily Tomlin's "Ernestine," and Julia Child. "Then my voice changed, and I could only do Julia Child. I had to work from there." He idolized David Frye.

"I remember one high school teacher allowed me five minutes of class time every day, if I wanted it, to stand up at the beginning of the class and get it out of my system." So Morris would do imitations of classmates, teachers, and even the principal. "One time I actually went on the public address system as the principal and dismissed the whole school early." Did the kids leave school? "Well, let's put it this way, everybody else left a lot earlier than I did that day."

During George H.W. Bush's four years as president it's safe to say Jim Morris and Dana Carvey were the hands-down best at impersonating him, and it would seem they took similar paths in mastering the voice. Carvey once said, "The way to do the president is to start out with Mister Rogers—'it's a beautiful day in the neighborhood'—then you add a little John Wayne—'here we go over the ridge.' You put them together, you've got George Herbert Walker Bush."

Asked how he developed Bush's voice, Morris said, "I suppose it was a cross between John Wayne and Mister Rogers and Liberace."

"We both captured the essence of the fellow," Morris told the *Boston Globe*. Dana Carvey "makes a bit more of a cartoon out of the guy, which sells comedy really well, and I think that I pick up the subtleties a little bit better."

Morris believes in drilling down beyond the most obvious traits. "It's like Jimmy Carter with a smile or with the rabbit, or Jerry Ford stumbling down the stairs," he explains. "Once you do the joke, then what? So I'm fascinated by news, and by politicians, and why people would even get into a life like that. So, really, I try to do what an editorial cartoonist might do. And that is take the news of the day and put a caption at the bottom. I'm like a walking, talking political cartoon."

At the Correspondents' Dinner in 1989:
I oppose abortion! Unborn humans have rights. They do. That is until they're born. Then they have the right to remain silent.

Morris says it was challenging to do the routine with the president and his wife, Barbara, seated just a few feet away. "I was very nervous, but not because I was performing for the president. It was more like, I was nervous about whether I was going to pull any punches and not go for the jugular. And I said, 'Well, what the hell? You only go around once.' And I hit him with the hardest hitting material I had and it was a success. That's what I do. I don't need to water it down for anybody."

Despite his success—and praise he received from Bush himself—Morris concedes that his work was never as widely appreciated as what Dana Carvey did week after week on SNL. "It gets more difficult when you consider that so many millions more people see and identify with [Carvey's] impression of the president than mine," he explains. "So a lot of times people will think that I'm going to come out with 'Wouldn't be prudent.' I don't do that in my act, but I'm not offended when people say, 'Oh, you're the guy who does that, right?' No. Not right."

◆ ◆ ◆

JON LOVITZ'S VIEW WAS PRESCIENT on election night: Dana Carvey would do dozens of cold opens as Bush on SNL. Toward the end of his term the portrayal got more teeth. For instance, during the Gulf War in 1990...

As commander in chief, I am ever cognizant of my authority to launch a full-scale orgy of death there in the desert sands. Probably won't. But, then again, I might.

(He gestures awkwardly for ten full seconds)

Now, if we do go to war, I can assure you it will not be another Vietnam. Because we have learned well the simple lesson of Vietnam: Stay out of Vietnam.

Franken and Downey were writing that sketch when one of the newer writers, Bob Odenkirk, walked by and gave them the Vietnam kicker, which got a huge audience response.

A few months later, Carvey switched Bush's focus to financial news...

The economy is a bit soft. Notice I didn't say recession. Not afraid to say recession. Recession. Recession. Recession. Heck, I'll say it all day, but I don't have to, because we're not in a recession. (Gestures) We're not even in a downturn, we're in more of a hovering action there.

Franken says the scripts were good, but Carvey's added touches were even better—so much so that they sometimes distracted from the principal gag that writers were aiming for. "We had to tell Dana between dress rehearsal and the show, 'Don't get so many laughs,' which I don't think anyone has ever told a performer."

♦ ♦ ♦

GEORGE H.W. BUSH LOST his 1992 re-election bid in an unusual three-way race with Bill Clinton and Texas businessman Ross Perot. Clinton got 45 million votes, Bush 39 million, and Perot a remarkable total of nearly 20 million. Dana Carvey did Perot on SNL, once playing both Bush and Perot in a '92 debate sketch. The Perot pieces were pre-taped and in the live show cast member David Spade was dressed as Perot in the wide shots.

Franken: "My favorite joke in the piece was a slightly surreal moment when each candidate looks at one of the others and we see what they're seeing. Bush looks at Clinton and sees him in long hair and headband smoking pot. Clinton looks over at Bush and sees him dressed as a prim little old lady. Bush and Clinton look over at Perot and see one of the Munchkins from the Lollipop Guild. There's nothing like trenchant satire!"

Soon after the election, Carvey was speaking with Jon Lovitz when a call came from the White House. "Suddenly I'm on the phone with President Bush," says Carvey. "I'm more than a bit nervous." Seems Bush was hoping to spread some cheer at his final staff Christmas party and thought Carvey would make a wonderful surprise guest. A few days later, Carvey and his wife, Paula, unpacked their bags in the Lincoln Bedroom. The staff party would be the following day, but on this night Bush hosted the Carveys and another couple for cocktails. "Hey Dana, why don't you do that impression you do of me for everybody right here, right now," said Bush. "I froze," recalls Carvey. "Suddenly my impression seemed like a grotesque representation of the actual man." But Bush egged him on, saying, "Don't tell me you're na ga da it." So Carvey called a Secret Service agent, fooling him into thinking he was speaking with the president.

The following day "Hail to the Chief" was played at the big Christmas gathering and Carvey walked in, was quickly recognized, received rousing applause (and probably would have gotten a standing ovation had the guests not already been on their feet). Then Bush strolled in, taking bows like a Broadway producer. Carvey told about being surprised by the invitation. He did some Bush and a bit of Perot. Barbara Bush spoke briefly, "Isn't he lucky I didn't hit him right on the head?" Then President Bush...

Dana's given me a lot of laughs. He said on the phone, 'You sure you really want me to come there?' And I said, 'yeah.' He said, 'I hope I've never crossed the line.' And I knew exactly what he meant. As far as I'm concerned, he never has. The fact that we can laugh at each other is a very fundamental thing. I'm not sure on November 4th that the invitation would have gone out with the same enthusiasm, but we're shifting gears. He's given us a wonderful kickoff to what I hope will be a joyous, totally friendly, very happy, somewhat nostalgic, merry Christmas for everybody.

Years later, Al Franken summed up Bush, the man, this way: "Can you imagine Donald Trump inviting Alec Baldwin to the White House?"

9 / *You gonna finish those fries?*

O n a Thursday in March, 1994, White House staffers gathered in the Roosevelt Room to celebrate Vice President Al Gore's 46th birthday. The boss, Bill Clinton, couldn't attend, but he delivered greetings via speakerphone. Genuinely touched, Gore said several times, "Thank you, Mr. President." Before hanging up Clinton declared, "One more thing. Keep your grubby little hands off my desk while I'm in California!"

The room erupted with laughter. The voice on the phone had been that of Jim Morris—happy to oblige when asked by Gore's aides to pull a phone prank. Gore, himself, was so pleased he invited Morris to the White House and a few weeks later escorted him into the Oval Office to meet Clinton. "The president was sitting at his desk reading," Morris recounted for me. "At first he didn't even look up, so I just went into my George H.W. Bush impression. I was strutting around the Oval saying things like, 'I had that painting on the other wall' and 'Oh, look, there's the stain we couldn't get out of the carpet from Billy Carter's days here.' Clinton's face got all red, and he was speechless. Cabinet members started coming in and there was no explaining what

Jim Morris as Bill Clinton.

was going on, so I went into my Bill Cinton impression. I felt such a rush.

"As I was leaving George Stephanopoulos walked in, and I was still doing Clinton and I said, 'George, you need a shave.' And he said, 'I always need a shave, Mr. President.' It was surreal."

For Jim Morris, doing Clinton for Clinton in the Oval Office was "like playing in the World Series." But for others the '90s weren't always so smooth.

◆ ◆ ◆

TUMULT DOESN'T BEGIN TO DESCRIBE Bill Clinton's eight years as president, or the lives of two extraordinarily gifted performers who impersonated him on "Saturday Night Live." The 42nd president faced a scandal involving the White House travel office, an investigation concerning a land deal in Arkansas, a charge of sexual harassment by a state clerical worker, and impeachment over an illicit affair with a White House intern about which he lied to federal investigators. Plus, he had a fondness for junk food, particularly from McDonald's. Remarkably, Clinton's approval rating climbed as high as 73 percent, and he was ultimately acquitted on impeachment charges and allowed to serve out his second term. Following the verdict, he told the nation: "I want to say again to the American people how profoundly sorry I am for what I said and did to trigger these events and the great burden they have imposed on the Congress and on the American people."

As for the SNL cast members, Phil Hartman, who rose to fame with his Clinton impression, was shot and killed by his wife in a brutal murder-suicide. Darrell Hammond, who skillfully took over the Clinton role, was treated for alcohol and drug addiction, self-mutilated with a blade nearly 50 times, and was stricken during a rehearsal by a panic attack so severe he had to be removed in a straight jacket.

◆ ◆ ◆

BELOVED PEOPLE ARE OFTEN ELEVATED IN DEATH, especially when their life is cut short in gruesome fashion. Lorne Michaels said of Phil Hartman, "He has done more work that's touched greatness than probably anybody else who's ever been here." SNL cast member Jan Hooks nicknamed Hartman "The Glue," because he seemed to hold the ensemble group together during difficult times.

In the wee hours of May 28, 1998, Hartman was shot three times at close range as he slept in his Encino, California home. Then...

The shooter, his third wife, Brynn, drives to a friend's house, leaving the couple's two sleeping children behind. High on cocaine and alcohol she confesses to the crime, but the friend, Ron Douglas, is in disbelief. Several hours later the two drive to the Hartman home, where Douglas discovers Phil's body and calls police. Brynn locks herself in the bedroom and phones her sister Kathy in Wisconsin. "Phil is dead!" she exclaims. "Tell the children that I love them." Police and other friends arrive at the residence and take the children to safety. A single gunshot rings out from the bedroom. Brynn, lying next to her husband, is dead.

Author Mike Thomas, who spent three years researching Hartman's life for the book "You Might Remember Me," writes, "I tried to understand and present him as much more than a highly gifted and widely beloved comic performer, or the still-mourned victim of a terrible crime. He was and is all of those, certainly, but he was also a deeply sensitive man who loved life and reveled in its nature; an eminently approachable and even gregarious public figure who was privately reserved and enigmatic; a loyal friend and generous collaborator."

♦ ♦ ♦

LIKE A SURPRISING NUMBER OF NOTABLES covered here so far—Rich Little, Jim Carrey, Dan Akyroyd and Lorne Michaels—Phil Hartmann (he later dropped the second "n" in his name) was born in Canada, the fourth of eight children. His father, Rupert, a traveling salesman, moved the family to Maine when Phil was eight and soon after that to California. Phil was a mediocre student but had skill as an artist and showed flashes of acting ability. Like many other comics-to-be he latched on to a favorite performer, memorized his record albums and then performed the routines for friends and family. Hartman's guy was Jonathan Winters, a man of many voices and strange sounds, who released seven LPs during the sixties. With a dash of Winters-style whimsy, Phil and a female classmate at Westchester High School were voted Class Clowns.

After dropping out of college, Hartman went to work at a music company owned by his older brother John, and designed album covers for groups such as America, Poco and Crosby, Stills & Nash. He also landed the lead as Professor Harold Hill in a production of "The Music Man" at Santa Monica's Morgan-Wixson Theater. Most consequentially, he joined the Groundlings improv group—at various times home to SNL's Laraine Newman, Jon Lovitz, Will Ferrell, Will Forte, Maya Rudolph and Kristen Wiig. Rather than pay the troupe's membership fee, he redesigned its logo.

One of the emerging artists at the Groundlings was Paul Reubens who, with Hartman's help, went on to create the character Pee-wee Herman. Hartman played bit parts and wrote scenes for the Pee-wee projects. His odd way of looking at things matched the character, as with a monologue Hartman wrote for Reubens in the film "Pee-wee's Big Adventure": "There's a lotta things about me you don't know anything about, Dottie. Things you wouldn't understand. Things you couldn't understand. Things you shouldn't understand."

In November 1985 Reubens hosted "Saturday Night Live," entirely as Pee-wee. Hartman and Groundlings alum John Paragon were hired to create material, for which they each received

$1,750. (This sort of arrangement is not unusual at SNL, where guests sometimes bring in a writer for a week. Barry Blaustein, for example, told me that he rejoined SNL whenever Eddie Murphy was on the show.) Six months later, Hartman returned to Studio 8H for his own audition and landed a job he described as being the show's Mr. Potato Head. "When you're so average looking," he said in an interview with Bob Costas, "when they put a wig on you and some glasses, if you alter your face and your voice in any way, you can look a lot different." Along with Dana Carvey and Jan Hooks, Hartman helped revitalize SNL, which had slumped and faced possible cancellation. Lorne Michaels called his new group "a charmed cast."

◆ ◆ ◆

BILL CLINTON WAS ONLY 32 when he became Governor of Arkansas in 1979, and at age 46 was the youngest president since JFK (who was 43). Like Kennedy, Clinton had charisma that translated well on screen—he was one of the first presidents to appear on latenight television, famously playing his saxophone on "The Arsenio Hall Show" in '92. His raspy Southern drawl was almost as catchy as Kennedy's Boston twang. He had a plethora of personal problems for impressionists to exploit and, as noted earlier, comedians have an easier time with personality traits than matters of policy—especially in TV parodies. With new sketch shows popping up on cable as well as on broadcast TV, and with the internet evolving as a major communications tool, Clinton impressions were everywhere.

As the 1992 election drew near, with Dana Carvey holding a firm grip on the role of President George H.W. Bush, Hartman developed his Clinton impression. By then Hartman had also become a regular on the animated hit series "The Simpsons," was making regular appearances with Jay Leno on the "Tonight Show," and had signed a deal with NBC that would give him a crack at his own prime-time series. But as his friend Carvey told him, if Clinton were to win in '92, it would "really put you on the map."

Eleven days after Clinton's victory, SNL's cold open showed Bush phoning contributors to apologize for the loss. ("I should have recognized the recession earlier. Didn't think it was prudent at this juncture.") An aide reminds Bush that Clinton is about to appear on television.

DON PARDO: *Ladies and gentlemen, the President-elect of the United States.*

CLINTON (Hartman): *Live from New York, it's Saturday Night!*

BUSH (Carvey): *I used to say that.*

And so the torch was passed. Hartman went on to do Clinton 18 times on SNL including a sketch soon after the election that revealed Hartman's hooks for the character and set a standard for performers who would do Clinton. The setting was a McDonald's in Washington. Clinton enters dressed in a University of Arkansas sweatshirt and Georgetown cap, accompanied by two Secret Service agents in jogging clothes...

CLINTON: *All right boys, let's stop here for a second. I'm a little parched from the jog.*

AGENT (Kevin Nealon): *Sir, we've only been jogging for three blocks. Besides, Mrs. Clinton asked us not to let you*

Jan. 16-22   89¢

TV GUIDE

HOW TO BE A "FUNNY PRESIDENT

The real transition is at *Saturday Night Live*—

How Phil does Bill...

...and why Dana's gonna miss George

ALSO:
HANGIN' WITH MR. CURRY

CABLE'S HOTTEST STARS

THE CLINTONS' FIRST FRIENDS

Dana Carvey and Phil Hartman Do Their Thing

in any more fast-food places.

CLINTON: *Well, I just want to mingle with the American people—talk with some real folks. And, maybe get a Diet Coke or something.*

AGENT: *Fine. But please don't tell Mrs. Clinton.*

CLINTON: *Jim, let me tell you something. There's going to be a lot of things we don't tell Mrs. Clinton about. Fast food is the least of our worries.*

The sketch remains one of SNL's best presidential put-downs. Clinton moseys over to a table to chat with a woman holding a baby. ("Say, you gonna finish these fries?") He sits down with the owner of a hardware store and his son. ("I see your boy doesn't like pickles.") Finishing the pickles, Clinton shakes hands with the restaurant manager. ("Is it too late for an Egg McMuffin?") A college student steps over to explain her problem with tuition. ("Say, that's one of those McLean sandwiches isn't it?") After taking a bite, he washes it down with some of the woman's milk shake, just as the manager arrives with the Egg McMuffin. Soon Clinton is explaining the situation in Somalia while tasting one patron's Chicken McNuggets and another's Filet 'O Fish. The problem, he says, is that warlords are intercepting food shipments. With that he pilfers a McDLT and hot apple pie and then reaches for a woman's McRib sandwich. Excitedly, Clinton asks, "Can I get a Coke?"

> AGENT: *Sir, I think we should probably continue your jog. We've only gone about an eighth of a mile.*
> CLINTON: *All right, all right. You guys up for a real run?*
> AGENTS: *Yes, Sir.*
> CLINTON: *Race you to the Pizza Hut!*

Following that sketch, Hartman was quoted as saying, "The whole nature of show business changed. I didn't have to go out and look for work anymore. Work came to me."

Soon Hartman had his own custom Clinton wig made, like the one he wore on SNL, so he could earn hefty paychecks doing corporate gigs, as Carvey had done during Bush's term. Unlike Bush, however, the real Bill Clinton didn't care much for

SNL's comedic portrayal. Hartman said he was shut out of White House events and other official functions. After meeting Clinton briefly at a New York charity event, Hartman told David Letterman, "I found out the hard way that he really doesn't like what I do."

Phil Hartman left SNL after eight seasons, at the top of his game. By then he had four luxury cars, a yacht and a $50,000 per episode deal with NBC to star in his own series, "NewsRadio." Four years later, at age 49, he was shot dead. His brother John wrote a poem for the funeral:

There lays a puzzle upon the bed
Where a pair of bloods have run out red.
She placed her rubies upon his head
To eclipse the life and light be shed
The night our shooting stars fell dead.

♦ ♦ ♦

BILL CLINTON WAS BECOMING the most parody-ripe president since Nixon, but with Hartman gone SNL had no one to play him. An SNL producer named Marci Klein (daughter of designer Calvin Klein), saw a little-known comic perform at Caroline's in mid-Manhattan. At 39, the guy was older than most struggling wannabes and he didn't do many impressions. However, his act included one sentence delivered as Bill Clinton: "I want to say to the people of America and the nations of the world, I hate you."

Klein arranged for Darrell Hammond to audition in Studio 8H before an audience consisting primarily of Lorne Michaels.

Trying to come up with as many impressions as possible for the 10-minute appearance, Hammond did a bit of Clinton and also Phil Donahue speaking Spanish. He was called back a week later and tried Ted Koppel speaking German. Michaels arranged for him to do a short set at the Comic Strip, where five years earlier the manager had turned him down, saying he lacked the "it" factor. This time Hammond killed, and was signed for SNL where he would portray Bill Clinton a remarkable 84 times.

◆ ◆ ◆

　　　DARRELL HAMMOND WAS THE TOUGHEST INTERVIEW I did for this book. His childhood story isn't just sad, it's chilling. He was literally tortured by his mother: hit on the head with a ball-peen hammer, stabbed and shocked with electric current. To placate his mother he did impressions of Popeye and Porky Pig, but the escape was temporary. In his memoir, "God, If You're Not Up There, I'm F*cked," Hammond writes about growing up in Melbourne, Florida, overwhelmed by fear:

> When the sun started to go down in the late afternoon, I was filled with foreboding, and everything was scary— the walls, the furniture, the rug, the very air was scary. I'd hear the branches of the hibiscus bush outside the kitchen window thump thump against the glass and feel something was coming to get me.

　　　Before he was 20 Hammond began cutting himself and was institutionalized repeatedly, taking as many as seven prescription drugs at a time. He drank heavily. It wasn't until many years and 23 different psychiatrists later that he was diagnosed as a trauma patient—unable to shed the memories of an awful childhood.

By the time he arrived at SNL his condition was controlled with a cocktail of prescription drugs "whose purpose was to stabilize a trauma patient enough that I could go out there." He drank on Saturday mornings but insists he was always sober during shows. "When the drinking didn't work, I cut myself. The wound created a fresh crisis to get me out of the one in my head." The cuts sometimes placed him in NBC's infirmary and even in the hospital. "I should have gotten myself an E-ZPass to the ER at New York Hospital, I was there so much."

Hammond's story has proved enlightening, even inspirational, for many people battling emotional problems. It's the basis of a moving 2019 documentary, "Cracked Up," in which director Michelle Esrick examines the biological effects of childhood trauma.

When we spoke, Hammond seemed exhausted by not only his life experiences but also the obligation to recount them so often. He brightened up when asked about doing over 100 characters on SNL, including Dick Cheney, Sean Connery, Regis Philbin—and most notably President Bill Clinton.

◆ ◆ ◆

"I WAS HAVING TROUBLE DOING HIM," Hammond said about his initial efforts with Clinton. "There were vowel sounds he made that I had no reference for. I noticed that he put his commas in illogical places. And I noticed that John F. Kennedy did something similar. So I go back to Ted Sorensen's JFK inaugural address, and I started doing that in a Southern accent. Then

I remembered that Arkansas is above Louisiana and Louisiana vowels are different from the vowels I've heard, because there's such a French quality to the way they pronounce certain vowels, so I took the Bayou aspect and then the JFK aspect and gradually it started to come together."

Can you compare or contrast your Clinton with Phil Hartman's approach?

"I don't want to compare and contrast. He did a great job and he was a great artist. I think great artists sometimes look at the same picture and see different things. ... I started looking at tapes of Clinton in the morning, tapes of him in the afternoon and evening. I noticed his voice changed during the day because a guy that talks a lot, his voice is going to get tired. So towards the end of the day, he developed a slight rasp in his voice. And that was the thing I took down to the Cellar in Greenwich Village to practice." So determined was Hammond to nail Clinton that he would do the character on SNL, and then experiment the following week with different approaches in front of a small club audience.

"He was the most complicated creature I've ever seen—a guy with 37 hand gestures when the rest of the world has three. So I had to congeal it somehow in a way that made sense to audiences. I had seen him bite his lip and I'd seen him do thumbs up. So one night I did those two things at the same time (at the Cellar) and the room kind of exploded. That was the thing that symbolized Clinton to them."

Hammond says he's never seen Clinton do both actions at the same time, but combined in his portrayal—referred to in SNL scripts as "The Clinton thumb and lip thing"—the character came alive. "People feel okay laughing at character- driven stuff," he explained. "They feel like they don't have to choose sides as a Democrat or Republican."

That pivotal remark underscores the evolution of presidential parodies on SNL and across most media. It's an issue we'll return to later. For Darrell Hammond, it was summarized this way:

"I was trying to be funny. Not to make a point."

President Clinton appeared to look more kindly on Hammond's work than that of Phil Hartman. When Clinton had knee surgery in 1997 and was temporarily on crutches, he invited Hammond to be his "clone" and share a speaking obligation at the Radio-Television Correspondents' Association Dinner [often confused with the White House Correspondents' Dinner, which in '97 was held a few weeks later]. Clinton spoke briefly, then

Hammond and Clinton rehearse before the dinner.

brought on Hammond, who wore his Clinton wig and makeup. Hammond's remarks were written entirely by the White House staff, yielding lines such as, "The key to being a clone is makin' sure you're the clone of somebody cool."

As Bill Clinton's legal problems mounted, SNL presented a cold open with Hammond speaking from the Oval Office. Will Ferrell, playing prosecutor Kenneth Starr, bursts in...

STARR: *Are you Darrell Hammond?*

CLINTON: *What? Who are you?*

STARR: *Are you Darrell Hammond, the man who plays the president on Saturday Night Live?*

CLINTON: *Yes.*

STARR: *Well, Mr. Hammond, my name is Kenneth Starr. I'm the independent counsel and I'm serving you with this subpoena. Come with me.*

CLINTON: *No. What do you want with me? I'm not the president.*

STARR: *Shut your hole Hammond. I've subpoenaed all the real people, now I'm subpoenaing the people who do impressions of them.*

(Agents drag Hammond out.)

STARR: *I'm going to enjoy this. Live from New York, it's Saturday Night!*

◆ ◆ ◆

IN 1996 BILL CLINTON'S SALARY AS POTUS was $200,000. That year Tim Watters, a real estate agent from Florida, earned $1.7 million as a Clinton impersonator, doing as many corporate gigs as he could handle—177 in all. Watters just happens to look like Clinton, so much so that soon after the '92 election he began doing meet-and-greets and photo-ops for relatively small fees. One appearance, at a Motorola business conference, caught the attention of promoter Randy Nolen, who saw a bigger potential. He signed Watters and spent $2,000 to buy jokes for him from comedian T.P. Mulrooney. They tested the act at a club called Zanies in St. Charles, Illinois, and soon were landing full-length corporate appearances for $10,000 and up. The material was soft, formulaic stuff, designed to play equally well for both conservative and liberal audiences. As in...

CLINTON: *Hillary and I make a point of going out for two romantic dinners each week. I go out on Mondays and Fridays and she goes out on Tuesdays and Saturdays. ... We have a beautiful two-story home in Chappaqua, N.Y. Usually, she'll have her story and I'll have mine. ... These days Hillary wears the pants in our family, which is good because often I can't locate mine.*

Soon Watters was making regular appearances on "The Tonight Show" with Jay Leno. He even portrayed Clinton in several movies, including "Naked Gun 33: The Final Insult" and "Austin Powers: The Spy Who Shagged Me." Watters nailed Clinton about as well as anyone ever has, but without the buzz that comes with being a regular on "Saturday Night Live" he never approached the notoriety of Phil Hartman or Darrell Hammond.

◆ ◆ ◆

DOING CLINTON ATTRACTED SO MANY PERFORMERS that even the great David Frye returned to the fray with a 1998 comedy album titled "Clinton: An Oral History." Back in the '60s

Frye's Lyndon Johnson and Richard Nixon set the standard for presidential impersonations, and his work was cited more often by comedians and writers I interviewed than anyone else's. I was eager to find his Clinton album and managed to acquire a used CD through Amazon. Though I don't often quote Amazon reviews, here's what verified purchaser "modbantam" had to say: "I have it on CD in the truck, and it's ok for a couple-chuckles... tops, and I am being generous. You will live a full happy life without it."

First, and most regrettably, Frye didn't do a very good job with Clinton's voice. Also, for most of its 39 minutes the material is almost entirely focused on Clinton's sexual dalliances—thus the unsubtle title—which would be easier to swallow (as Frye and his writers might have said) were it funny. Samples:

> Q: *President Clinton, have you ever led men in uniform into battle?*
> CLINTON (Frye): *Well, I once sent a couple of state troopers to the liquor store. Gennifer loves her Kahlua. ...*
> AL GORE (Frye): *We have reluctantly decided to give our commander-in-chief a choice—impeachment or castration. I hope the president doesn't look at this as losing his manhood as much as the country gaining two first ladies. ...*
> CLINTON: *Government has no place in the bedroom. Neither does the media. So all I can say is, "Kiss my big white Arkansas ass."*

♦ ♦ ♦

CLINTON WAS ALSO AN EASY TARGET for the low-brow sketch shows that sprouted during the '90s. One of the first of these irreverent offerings was "In Living Color," which ran for five seasons on the Fox network. The cast was led by Jim Carrey, who portrayed George H.W. Bush for two years, then segued to doing Clinton in '92. Carrey's first effort, just before the election, had Clinton at a news conference which turns into a song-and-dance number called "Humpin' Around (Too Much Lust to Trust)," a spoof of the Bobby Brown hit...

CLINTON: *When you trust someone*
And then you say he lied.
You believe it was Gennifer Flowers,
And you claim that I am not qualified
Because I work that booty for hours.
I'm not a draft dodger.
No, not like that fool Quayle.
No, don't believe the things they say.
I am not an adulterer, and I did not inhale.
So vote for me on Election Day.

Carrey's Clinton was not precise, but the edgy satire was reminiscent of "That Was the Week That Was," which skewered Lyndon Johnson with similar brashness in the '60s.

A few days before Clinton's inauguration, Carrey was back with another song, this one based on the "Beverly Hillbillies," or "The Capital Hillbillies" as the sketch called it...

Come and listen to a story 'bout a man named Bill,
Hick Razorback with a destiny to fill.
But 20 years before he would take the oath and freed,

He dodged Vietnam and he toked a little weed.
Reefer that is. Mary Jane. Didn't inhale.

By the time the song ends, Clinton is in the Oval Office with Gennifer Flowers on his lap and "another redneck," Al Gore of Tennessee, at his side.

In 1995 Fox tried a new sketch show, "Mad TV," which ran on Saturday night, starting a half-hour before NBC's "Saturday Night Live." It was even more sophomoric than "In Living Color"—a difficult feat—and had its own way of dealing with President Clinton. The role went to cast member Will Sasso.

As he recalls: "One of our writer-producers, Brian Hartt, said, 'Can you do Clinton?' I was like, 'Yeah, I guess.' And then we were messing around and I said, 'It always seems like he's got gas. He always has a look on his face like he's about to burp.' So the first sketch we did was actually a thing called 'Gassy Clinton,' where he's making some speech somewhere, and he talks about eating sausages with the chancellor of Germany. And then throughout the sketch he keeps burping and, of course, in 'Mad TV' fashion, the last line was 'God bless America,' and then a long burp."

I asked Sasso if "Mad TV" was trying to turn up the heat more than SNL.

"Yeah, I think that was something that we had to do in order to be competitive, or have a hope of being competitive. Our thing was, we kind of pushed the envelope a little bit."

How did Clinton fit in?

"It just so happened that Bill Clinton played it a little fast and loose. He was like Slick Willy. He just didn't care. A guy who's got the nuclear codes but is more interested in, you know, going down on an intern or whatever. So it was very easy for us to translate that into any number of bizarre situations."

Do you think you swayed voters' opinions?

"If someone's vote is swayed by watching 'Mad TV' then have at it. No, I don't think so."

Did you ever hear from Clinton or anyone at the White House?

"No, never. After all, we weren't 'Saturday Night Live.'"

♦ ♦ ♦

DURING HIS TIME AT SNL Dana Carvey was the GOAT (Greatest of All Time) when he portrayed George H.W. Bush. But as Bill Clinton he became just... the goat. "I suck," he told *GQ*. "I couldn't do Clinton." Yet, after leaving NBC Carvey tried it—in prime-time no less—spoiling the premiere of ABC's "The Dana Carvey Show" and almost derailing his own career.

Produced by SNL alum Robert Smigel, the new Carvey show was given a coveted time slot, right after Tim Allen's hit family sitcom "Home Improvement." "It's not going to be an SNL clone," Smigel pledged. "We're going to really try to do inventive things." He hired a Hall of Fame staff that included Steve Carell, Stephen Colbert and Louis C.K., along with writers Jon Glaser, Charlie Kaufman, Robert Carlock and Bob Odenkirk.

Although the show lasted only seven weeks—with ratings and reviews so bad that the eighth show was pulled before its airdate—it had many hilarious moments. What the series couldn't overcome was Carvey's portrayal of Clinton in the opening sketch of the first show. The setting was the Oval

Office, with Carvey as Clinton talking to camera . . .

CLINTON: *Good evening my fellow Americans. As you know it's an election year and my wife Hillary Clinton has been the subject of numerous accusations, accusations which I believe are unfair. But screw it, she's history, I can't afford her. I've placed Hillary Clinton under house arrest. Now some of you may think this is cruel, but I'm not a cruel man. I'm a caring, nurturing president and without Hillary I can be both father and mother to our nation. This isn't just talk, I've taken this a step further. With the employment of estrogen hormonal therapy I have developed the ability to breast-feed. Let's just take a look here. Let me open up my shirt so you can see.*

Carvey exposes a prosthetic chest with eight nipples that squirt milk. He's handed a baby (doll) and begins breastfeeding. Then live puppies and kittens are brought in to join the milking.

Carvey's Clinton breastfeeds a baby and puppies.

Carvey turns to reveal he's also had a hen's rear added to his bottom so he can keep eggs warm in a nest that's been placed on his office chair.

"The president breastfeeding was probably the worst decision I've ever been involved in," said Smigel.

"When you see it in context," added Carvey, "it's just grotesque for a prime-time audience with kids."

That night ABC invested in minute-by-minute ratings. The data showed that during the Clinton sketch an estimated six million viewers tuned out, which might have been some kind of record.

Said Smigel, "We literally killed our show in the first five minutes."

Dana Carvey, of course, would rebound in his career and his impressions, and almost everyone connected with the failed ABC series moved on to more successful projects. Bill Clinton also survived—but if his successor had one thing over him, it was a genuine sense of presidential humor.

10 / *Strategery*

I t's Christmas 2002 at Prairie Chapel Ranch, the 1,600-acre spread near Crawford, Texas, owned by George and Laura Bush.

After dinner, as the family celebrates near the fire, Barbara Bush tells her son, George W, that she'd like him to watch a VHS tape. What soon flickers on the screen is a man whose voice and appearance are eerily similar to the president's. This doppelganger is actor Steve Bridges, portraying Bush in a video presentation that was played before Barbara Bush's appearance at a fundraiser for a private Christian school. The gist of what Bridges said as Bush: If I'd spent more time with schooling, I wouldn't have so many problems with public speaking.

The president loved the tape, which matched his taste in humor. Just a few weeks earlier his Scottish terrier, Barney, had conducted a dog's-eye tour of the White House in a four-and-half minute video that was shown by TV networks and became so popular online that it briefly crashed the White House website. So, George W's response to seeing Steve Bridges was to invite him to the Oval Office.

The meeting took place two months later, but not without additional intrigue. As Bridges's manager, Randy Nolen, explained it to me, an environmental group known as The Detroit Project—founded by progressives Ari Emanuel, Arianna Huffington and Larry David's then-wife Laurie—offered Bridges $25,000 to do a 30-second commercial. The group was advocating for cars powered by fossil fuel alternatives and the TV spot would make it seem as if Bush endorsed their efforts. A Christian conservative and a supporter of the president, Bridges not only turned it down, he and Nolen sent the script to senior White House advisor Karl Rove, alerting the administration to what The Detroit Project was up to.

When Bridges entered the Oval Office, Bush threw his arms around him and proceeded to conduct a 20-minute tour for Bridges, Nolen and Emmy-winning makeup artist Kevin

Promoter Randy Nolen, left, with Laura Bush, George W. Bush and actor Steve Bridges.

Haney, who was responsible for transforming Bridges into Bush for the video (not for this visit, however, as Bridges preferred to meet the president without the full getup).

Bush told his guests he'd like to make use of Bridges's remarkable talent, perhaps at the annual White House Correspondents' Dinner. However, with global tensions high—the U.S. would launch an invasion of Iraq just a few weeks later—four years would pass before it could be arranged.

♦ ♦ ♦

NERD PROM HAS A SIGNIFICANT PLACE in the history of presidential impersonations and roasting. As noted earlier, the 1989 event was a terrific showcase for Jim Morris and his George H.W. Bush routine, but the 1976 dinner was a train wreck for Chevy Chase's Gerald Ford. A few months after George W. Bush took office in 2001, the WHCD featured SNL's Darrell Hammond, who wrote of being so nervous that "I had strategically consumed a bottle of wine beforehand."

On stage, Hammond began: "Despite what I do for a living and where I do it, it's an honor and a privilege to perform for the president of the United States. That said..."

The audience roared at the suggestion that some Bush bashing would ensue—but Hammond only referred to the new president once in 26 minutes. ("I read that the first time you met with the Chinese ambassador you brought your laundry.") He did spend several minutes imitating Bush's predecessor, Bill Clinton, and even more time doing the man Bush narrowly defeated, Al Gore. Of course, Clinton and Gore were Hammond's specialties on SNL, but the dearth of Bush material this night was surprising.

By 2006, with Bush's approval ratings dipping to 36 percent, the White House extended an invitation to Steve Bridges to appear at April's WHCD. Comedy writer Landon Parvin, hired by the Bush family, and Evan Davis, working for Randy Nolen, collaborated on the script, which Bush and Bridges rehearsed the day before in the White House theater. "The president walked in and he had his lines totally memorized," recalls Nolen. "Steve was nervous. He was the guy who didn't know the script."

With more than 2,000 people in attendance at the Washington Hilton, two identical podiums with presidential seals were placed center stage. Bridges would pretend to voice Bush's inner thoughts. Some excerpts . . .

BUSH: *Members of the White House Correspondents' Association, distinguished guests, ladies and gentlemen.*

BRIDGES: *Here I am. Dang press dinners. Could be home asleep. Little Barney curled up at my feet. But no, I gotta pretend I like being here. (pause) The media really ticks me off the way they try to embarrass me by not editing what I say.*

BUSH: *I'm absolutely delighted to be here, as is Laura.*

BRIDGES: *She's hot. Muy caliente.*

BUSH: *As you know I always look forward to these dinners.*

BRIDGES: *It's just a bunch of media types. Hollywood liberals. Democrats like Joe Biden. How come I can't have dinner with the 36% of the people who like me?*

BUSH: *Let's talk about some serious issues such as...*

BRIDGES: *Okay, here it comes. Nuclear proliferation. Nuclear proliferation. Nuclear proliferation.*

BUSH: *Nukier perliberation.*

BRIDGES: *All right, maintain. Be cool. Let's give this a try: We must enhance non compliance protocols. Sanction not only at IAEA formal sessions, but through intersessional contact.*

BUSH: *We must enhance noncompliance protocols. Sanction not only at ee-aye, ee-aye, oh formal sessions, but through intersexual conduct.*

BRIDGES: *Some of my critics in the international community call me arrogant. I will not even honor that with a response. Screw 'em. (pause) Nah, don't say screw 'em, let's hit them with some rhetorical eloquence.*

BUSH: *My friends, our purple mountains with ramparts red glare, white with foam and justice for all fruity plains gallantly streaming from sea to shining sea with a shining city on a shining hill above a shining prairie and maybe some shiny trees and a few shrubs I see a shiny America.*

BRIDGES: *We can all come together.*

BUSH: *As most of my predecessors have known, it's really important to be able to laugh in this job. And I thank you for giving us the chance to laugh tonight. ... God bless our troops. God bless the cause of freedom. And God bless America. Thank you.*

It was a healthy dose of self-deprecation by a sitting president, and a remarkable impersonation by Steve Bridges. [When

Bush and Bridges go for laughs in Washington.

I transcribed the video using Otter software, the program was unable to distinguish which man was speaking and attributed everything to a single voice.]

Though Bridges did not receive money for the appearance, Nolen says Bush told him backstage, "This is going to be good for you guys." Indeed, it was. "Shortly afterwards," according to Nolen, "we got a call to do the Barbra Streisand tour and did 19 out of 20 shows with her. We got our full fee for it. Steve was booked solid for the next six months at $35,000 per show. I couldn't take any more days, we had so many that we just couldn't get to them."

Seeking to expand his repertoire, Bridges developed a Bill Clinton impression, which was quite good, and then a Barack Obama portrayal which was weak. "'The Tonight Show' put Steve on once as Obama," Nolen recounts, "but they felt uncomfortable with a white actor playing a Black president."

In March, 2012, Bridges did three days of presidential impressions in Hong Kong for which he received a total of $100,000. Upon returning home to Los Angeles he suffered what was later determined to have been a severe allergic reaction. Steve Bridges, 48, was discovered dead by his housekeeper.

◆ ◆ ◆

THE 2000 BUSH-GORE CAMPAIGN was summed up by "Saturday Night Live" in two words: "strategery" and "lockbox."

On three successive Saturdays before Election Day, SNL presented debate sketches which, cumulatively, stand as perhaps television's best political satires. The genius behind the routines was writer Jim Downey, the veteran who joined SNL in its second season and stayed, on and off, for four decades. He's the half-brother of filmmaker Robert Downey Sr. and the uncle of actor Robert Downey Jr. His comedy career began in college as editor of the *Harvard Lampoon* and he arrived at SNL the same week as Bill Murray, with whom he shared an office. Downey's personal political views are tough to pin down, but his writing partner, Al Franken, considered him a conservative and, as such, a welcome balance to Franken's liberal views. One thing's certain: Downey was funny. In SNL's first 2000 debate...

JIM LEHRER (Chris Parnell): *Mr. Vice President, during this campaign, you have frequently called the Bush tax plan a risky scheme. Why?*

AL GORE (Darrell Hammond): *Well, Jim, Governor Bush and I have two very different plans to offer tax relief to American families. In his plan, the wealthiest 1 percent of Americans would receive nearly 50 percent of the benefits. My plan, Jim, is different. Rather than squander the surplus on a risky tax cut for the wealthy, I would put it in what I call a lockbox.*

LEHRER: *Governor Bush, your response.*

GEORGE W. BUSH (Will Ferrell): *I don't know what that was all about. But I will tell you this: Don't mess with Texas.*

GORE: *I didn't mess with Texas.*

LEHRER: *Governor Bush, I listened very carefully to the Vice President's remarks and I honestly do not believe he messed with Texas. Now, Governor Bush...*

GORE: *Jim, can I just add that in my plan, the lockbox would be used only for Social Security and Medicare. It will have two different locks. One of the keys to the lockbox will be kept by the president. The other key would be sealed in a small magnetic container and placed under the bumper of the Senate majority leader's car.*

...

LEHRER: *Which brings us to our final question. Governor Bush, both you and the Vice President have offered plans to provide prescription drugs for the elderly. What makes your plan superior?*

GORE: *Jim, I'd like to interrupt here and answer that question as if it were my turn to speak. Let me tell you about a friend of mine. Her name is Etta Munson. She's 94. She's a widow living on Social Security in Sparta, Tennessee. Etta was born with only one kidney. She also suffers from polio, spinal meningitis, lung, liver and pancreatic cancer, an enlarged heart, diabetes and a rare form of cystic acne. Now, several recent strokes along with an unfortunate shark attack have left her paralyzed and missing her right leg under the knee. Just last week, she awoke from a coma to find that due to a hospital mix up her left arm had been amputated, infected with syphilis, and then reattached.*

LEHRER: *Mr. Vice President, we are short of time.*

GORE: *As you can imagine, Jim, Etta's prescription drug bills are staggering. They run to nearly $113 million a day. Etta tells me that some weeks she has to choose between eating or treating her Lyme disease. Under my plan her prescription drugs would be covered. Under my opponent's plan her house would be burned to the ground. And that is wrong. That is just wrong.*

LEHRER: *Governor Bush, response.*

BUSH: *I believe that some of his figures may be inaccurate.*

GORE: *Jim, what you just heard from my opponent is*

an attack on my integrity and my character. But I will
not reply in kind. Instead, I will take those remarks and
put them away—away in a tiny lockbox, where all bad
thoughts go.
LEHRER: *Well, that brings us to the close of tonight's de-*
bate. Each candidate will now give a brief closing state-
ment.
GORE: *Jim, can I make two closing statements?*
LEHRER: *I'm afraid not. In fact, we are almost out of*
time. So I will instead ask each candidate to sum up in a
single word the best argument for his candidacy.
Governor Bush.
BUSH: *Strategery.*
LEHRER: Vice President Gore.
GORE: *Lockbox.*

Al Franken's take: "Will Ferrell's George W. Bush hilar-
iously captured what everyone already thought about Bush—
inarticulate, not particularly bright. Darrell Hammond's Al Gore,
as written by Downey, unfortunately crystallized what some
voters hadn't noticed—a tendency to be wonkish and somewhat
supercilious." In hindsight: "I was, and still am, a huge fan of
Gore's. I wish that Downey hadn't written this, because it may
have changed 500 votes in Florida. But it was a great piece of
writing."

◆ ◆ ◆

AT HIS SNL AUDITION Will Ferrell did a brief political
impression: Ted Kennedy attempting stand-up comedy. He also
provided a sample of his hilarious take on the legendary base-

ball announcer Harry Caray, but unlike the others who were evaluated that day by Lorne Michaels—Cheri Oteri and Chris Kattan—Ferrell didn't present himself as an impressionist per se. He did, however, have a keen sense of the weird. For his final audition piece he was a businessman sitting on the floor of his office playing with cat toys.

Here are some things you might not know about Will Ferrell, even if you've plotzed at his George W. Bush, Alex Trebek and other characters on SNL, and watched "Anchorman" and his other movies countless times...

He grew up in Irvine, California and was fascinated with Matchbox cars. His dad, Roy Lee Ferrell Jr., played saxophone and keyboard for the Righteous Brothers. His mother, Kay, was a teacher. Will Ferrell holds a degree in "sports information" from USC, where he graduated in 1989. His first job after college was as a parking attendant (once ripping the luggage rack off a van while trying to drive under a low beam). His second job was as a bank teller (short $300 the first day and $280 the next). He worked at NBC as an intern in the sports department. He played in five Major League spring training baseball games (his greatest accomplishment was fouling off a 92 mph pitch). *Autograph* magazine named him Worst Celebrity Autographer—for taunting fans while signing.

As the 2000 campaign took shape, Lorne Michaels offered Darrell Hammond his pick between Bush and Gore. Hammond opted for Gore, so Michaels turned to Ferrell and said, "Do you want to play Bush? You're tall." Ferrell's answer was, "Why not, he's not going to win."

In learning the part, "I just find one thing I can hang my hat on," Ferrell explained to a gathering at the Newseum in Washington. "And for Bush, for instance, I just knew he squinted his eyes a lot ... and then I got more comfortable with the voice ... If you could find one little tick you can build it." Ferrell also leaned on a phrase that helped cement the perception of Bush's down-home obliviousness: "Don't mess with Texas."

Although Bush was an easy target for character-focused jokes, his administration was marked by serious policy matters that Ferrell's routines had no choice but to address, such as the bombing of Iraq, darkly framed as a gesture to help Bill Clinton...

BUSH (Ferrell): *On Friday, February 16, at 12:30 p.m. Eastern Time, I ordered a surprise military strike against Iraq in order to move his latest scandals off the front pages. Now, let me make something very clear. There was utterly no legal or military just-er-fer-cation for this strike. Many innocent Iraqi civilians were killed or injured and the men and women of our armed forces were needlessly placed in harm's way. But if you look at your morning paper, you'll see the Mark Rich pardon story is on page five, which means ex-President Clinton can now get on with his life and enjoy this wonderful three-day weekend. ... Were Bill Clinton in my place, he would have done the same. Were he still president, he would have bombed Iraq to get his pardon of Mark Rich out of the news. I did it for him, because he would have done it for him. It's called bipartisanship. ... To Saddam Hussein: Don't mess with Texas.*

♦ ♦ ♦

FEW SITTING PRESIDENTS HAVE BEEN PORTRAYED in theatrical films. An early exception was the drama "PT 109," about John Kennedy's heroic efforts as a Naval officer serving in the South Pacific during World War II. Released just five months before Kennedy's death in 1962, the movie stars Cliff Robertson, who was personally selected by JFK to portray him (despite the fact that Jackie Kennedy reportedly wanted Warren Beatty to play the role). Produced by Warner Bros. with significant guidance from the White House, the film was limited exclusively to Kennedy's wartime experience, not his presidency.

Ten years later, two contemporaneous films, "Another Nice Mess" and "Richard," focused on Richard Nixon's presidency and were released during his time in office, but neither made much impact.

Oliver Stone's 2008 film "W." delivered a fact-based but clearly fictionalized version of the personality and politics of George W. Bush, while he was in office. Josh Brolin provided the Bush impersonation, having spent many hours studying the president's speech patterns and body language. However, according to the *Los Angeles Times*, "He wasn't trying to concoct a spitting-image impression, which ran the potential of becoming a 'Saturday Night Live' caricature. 'It's not for me to get the voice down perfectly,' (then) 40-year-old Brolin said, even though he came close. More important, the actor said, was to unearth Bush's inner voice—'Where is my place in this world? How do I get remembered?'"

That task was made more difficult by the fact that Bush

still occupied the Oval Office. The critic Manohla Dargis called Brolin's performance "incomplete" and noted in her *New York Times* review, "It can be disconcerting when actors play historical figures, and it's infinitely stranger when those figures aren't obscured by time. But it's one thing to watch Paul Giamatti scowling about in a presidential wig, as he did in the recent HBO mini-series 'John Adams.' It's something entirely different to watch Mr. Brolin sloppily downing drinks in a pantomime of the current president's younger self, a figure that doesn't belong to history but to the present and, by extension, to us. Good as he is, he can't touch the original."

Though Stone was no fan of Bush, "W." ultimately failed as a take-down for the same reason that many impersonations of both the father and son came up short. Portrayals that might have been intended to make them appear cartoonish instead enhanced their likability. The younger Bush, the cliché went, seemed to be a guy you'd like to have a beer with.

On the day Bush left office, January 20, 2009, Will Ferrell parachuted—or at least seemed to, thanks to a theatrical harness—onto the stage of the Cort Theatre in New York, for the first performance of "You're Welcome America. A Final Night with George W Bush." The limited engagement ran for two months, setting box office records, with Ferrell playing Bush for the last time (although he later reprised the role on TV). Directed by Ferrell's partner Adam McKay, it was an irreverent review of Bush's life and presidency. About his first day as president: "I remember thinking, shit, I actually have to do this now." Referring to Obama: "I'm a fan of the Tiger Woods guy. ... I don't hate Black people, I never even think about them." About Vice President Dick Cheney: "A guy so charismatic he could shoot a man in the face with a shotgun and have that guy apologize to him." Liberated after leaving office, he shows the theater audience a photo of his penis. The play ends with Bush sitting on the stage, drinking a Budweiser, and giving the audience the finger.

In an exit interview, Ferrell said about Bush: "I kind of feel like he's someone who—and I think this is documented—he is someone who is seeking acceptance throughout his entire life, and finally got into the most prominent position of power in the world, and then thought 'My way or the highway.' There are times when I was doing him and I thought, 'I kind of feel sorry for him.' But then I'd think, 'No, he's a grown man, he needs to be held accountable for what happened.'"

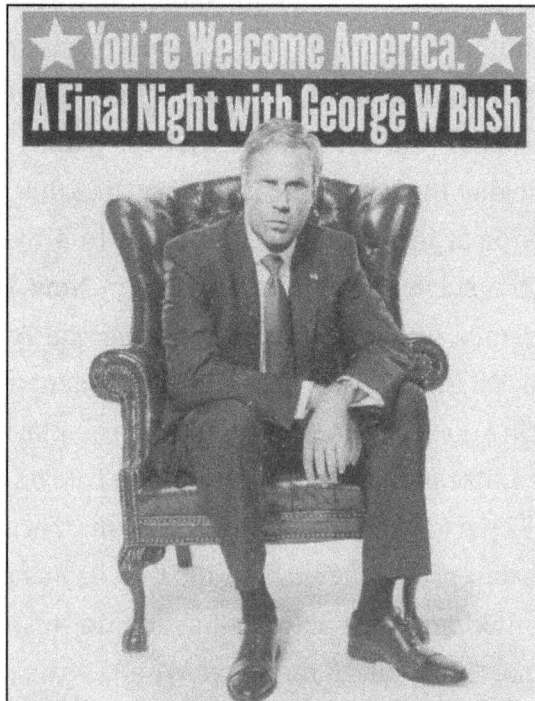

11 / *I'm a fun guy*

For many Americans, Barack Obama's election in 2008 was the most emotionally uplifting since Kennedy defeated Nixon in 1960, though few gushed about it quite the way Chris Matthews famously did on MSNBC: "I have to tell you ... the feeling most people get when they hear Barack Obama's speech. My, I felt this thrill going up my leg. I mean, I don't have that too often."

But while some pundits were thrilled, many entertainers were not. Chris Rock called Obama "a comedian's worst nightmare." Bill Maher observed, "On top of being perfect, he's Black, and liberals are afraid to laugh at anything with a Black person in it." Jim Downey, SNL's veteran political expert, said, "If I had to describe Obama as a comedy project, I would say, 'Degree of difficulty, 10 point 10.'" In the book "Live from New York," Downey reasoned, "It's like being a rock climber looking up at a thousand-foot-high face of solid obsidian, polished and oiled. There's not a single thing to grab onto—certainly not a flaw or hook that you can caricature."

Indeed, Obama had as much Teflon as Ronald Reagan,

but with the opposite effect. Comics and impressionists tried to damage Reagan but frequently failed, while most of them sought to shield Obama and usually succeeded. This was aided by the fact that political impressions and satire are almost exclusively the sports of liberals. The few conservative platforms for such material are so obscure as to be irrelevant. Greg Gutfeld has a comedy program on Fox News Channel and Mike Huckabee has a variety show, but who would ever compare them to Colbert, Oliver, Kimmel, Meyers, Fallon, etc.?

Eight months before the 2008 election SNL presented a faux debate between Obama and Hillary Clinton. Kristen Wiig, portraying CNN's Campbell Brown, began with a disclaimer for herself and her colleagues: "Like nearly everyone in the news media, the three of us are totally in the tank for Senator Obama." She described herself as an "Oba-maniac." The sketch was effective because it mocked journalists without even slightly damaging the senator from Illinois.

Obama was played by Fred Armisen...

For too long in this country the press has been hearing the same old refrain, 'Just give us the news, not your personal opinions.' And they're tired of it. They're tired of being told, 'You journalists have to stay neutral. You can't openly take sides in a political campaign." And they're saying, 'Yes we can. Yes we can take sides. Yes we can!

In its first show following the historic election, SNL didn't even attempt an Obama sketch, opting for a "speech" by newly elected Vice President Joe Biden, played by Jason Sudeikis. ("What's the difference between Joe Biden and a pitbull? You

Armisen, left, and Pharoah were easygoing Obamas.

can teach a pitbull to keep its mouth shut.") The sketch worked because it mocked Biden without knocking Obama.

"Saturday Night Live" was consistently soft on the 44th president, first with Armisen—highly skilled but miscast and not even Black—and then Jay Pharoah—at the time SNL's first new Black male cast member in seven years.

◆ ◆ ◆

JARED ANTONIO FARROW started doing impressions at age six, captivated by Gilbert Gottfried's Iago—the cartoon bird in "Aladdin" who could mimic other voices. Robin Williams was another early favorite, but Jared focused mostly on the relatively few Black impressionists who broke through with white audiences in the '50s and '60s. One was mega-star Sammy Davis Jr., the other a lesser-known impressionist named George Kirby. Then there was Eddie Murphy who, like Jared, made his first appearance as a professional impressionist at age 15. Murphy worked at small clubs within walking distance of the Brooklyn apartment where he was raised; Jared grew up in Virginia and followed his father's guidance in developing an act with the stage name Jay Pharoah.

At age 15 were adult audiences laughing at you or with you?

"I think they were laughing at me impersonating celebrities talking about a situation," he told me. "So I don't think they were laughing at me. I think they would just feel like yeah, this is kind of cool. He's talking about something, but he's doing it as somebody else."

He toured for a while with Eddie Murphy's brother, Charlie. In 2008, while studying business at Virginia Commonwealth University, Pharoah was urged by a friend to develop an Obama impression, which he performed at Funny Bone in Virginia Beach. Beyond nailing the voice, Pharoah stressed personality over politics, imagining Obama picking up girls in college...

Hey, you, over there. I said, hey you over there. Come here. I want to talk to you. I said, I want to talk to you. I've been noticing you. And I have to say that I really like it. So, let's just cut to the chase. In my dorm room I've got a bottle of Jack Daniels and all the chicken you can eat. And whatever happens, we can just blame it on the alcohol. Thank you! Thank you so much!

Pharoah's routine got over 2 million views on YouTube, which back then was a big deal, and it caught the attention of producers at "Saturday Night Live." He did Obama in his audition for Lorne Michaels and was hired at age 22, but sat on the bench for two seasons as Fred Armisen continued in the Obama role.

"Fred Armisen was, you know, definitely a seasoned performer, not to say that I wasn't," Pharoah recounts, "but he had stature and he was the one everybody was familiar with. You can't just unplug the machine like that, you kind of got to amicably switch the powers over."

Armisen played the part throughout Obama's first term, with sketches such as the cold open on April 24, 2010, that was an immediate contender for the least funny in SNL's history. In it Obama spoke about meeting with Wall Street leaders who rejected his plea for financial reforms but joined him for lunch at a New York restaurant where he enjoyed, "The best steak I have ever had in my life. The menu had 30 different kinds of cuttlefish. Thirty. I had no idea there were that many kinds of cuttlefish."

Producers were reluctant to switch to Pharoah and even less willing to be tough with Obama. The president got so little attention that Armisen was frequently featured in cold opens portraying Lawrence Welk, the corny bandleader who had left TV two decades earlier. Armisen did his final turn as Obama on May 12, 2012, in a sketch that, again, poked fun at Vice President Biden...

BIDEN (Jason Sudeikis): *Vice presidents never get to go anywhere.*

OBAMA (Armisen): *Joe, come on. You should be proud of what you did on "Meet the Press." You're a great vice president, Joe.*

BIDEN: *Well, some people say I'd make a great president. Better than you even.*

OBAMA: Who says that, Joe?

BIDEN: *George.*

OBAMA: *We're going to talk about your imaginary friend, George, again?*

BIDEN: *He's not imaginary. He's real.*

OBAMA: *Joe, we have one more campaign to get through and I need to know, can I count on you?*

BIDEN: *Yes.*

OBAMA: *I can't hear you.*

BIDEN: (mocking) *Yeeeessss!*

The dreadful sketch only turns funny when Armisen leaves the room and Will Ferrell enters as Biden's secret pal, "George" (W. Bush)...

BUSH (Ferrell): *If you'd been my vice we would have burned this city to the ground.*

BIDEN: *Literally or figuratively?*

BUSH: *What's the one where there's a real fire?*

Before Season 38, as Pharoah explains, "Lorne Michaels called me into his office and he said, 'We're gonna have you play Obama. I think you're ready to do it,'" and with that Pharoah took over—beginning with an artful handoff. With Pharoah in the Obama role, Armisen played a local politician at a rally in Ohio: "And now it is my distinct honor to introduce the President of the United States. I wouldn't want his job, right? Ladies and gentlemen, President Barack Obama." Pharoah entered and immediately established his feel for the character, with a series of thank yous and dialogue conveying the essence of no-drama Obama. And yet, the sequence succeeded primarily because it featured Sudeikis mocking Mitt Romney. At one point Obama croons, "I'm so in love with you," from the Al Green song "Let's Stay Together," while Romney entertains a conservative crowd with "E-I-E-I-O" from "Old MacDonald Had a Farm."

Even with a better impressionist in place, SNL did few sketches about Obama, and those that did run were tame.

Pharoah recalls, "Lorne came up to me at one point and said, 'You got to play Obama Presidential.' So all of the extra ticks that you could put in there, to give a view of his other side, it was kind of stopped a little bit." Pharoah got a chance to do his Obama for Obama during a private party hosted by Justin Timberlake and Jessica Biel. At a subsequent encounter, according to Pharoah, Obama told him, "You've got to have more fun with it, man. I like to have fun, Jay. I'm a fun guy."

◆ ◆ ◆

Pharoah and Obama share a laugh at a D.C. party.

Reggie Brown as Obama.

ARGUABLY THE MOST SUCCESSFUL Obama impressionist, and at times the most controversial, was Reggie Brown, who sounds and looks very much like Obama, especially when wearing a set of prosthetic ears. In 2012 he recorded an Obama parody video dancing and rapping to a track of Psy's K-pop hit "Gangnam Style," getting over 100 million views worldwide. According to Bloomberg News, millions of viewers in China believed the man gyrating on screen was the real U.S. president.

A year earlier, Brown had the distinction of being yanked off the stage while impersonating Obama at the Republican Leadership Conference for what were deemed "racially inappropriate" jokes. ("My father was a Black man from Kenya, and my mother was a white woman from Kansas. So, for the last time, yes, my mother loved a Black man and, no, she was not a

Kardashian.") Brown maintains that what really riled organizers was how he treated prominent Republicans. (About cancer
treatments for Newt Gingrich's wife: "You know the old saying,
'When the going gets rough, Newt files for divorce.'") His ouster
at the conference got Brown numerous TV appearances—including several on Bill Maher's HBO show—plus a full slate of
corporate gigs.

In the final years of Obama's presidency, Brown modified
his act, mixing a bit of humor with personal advice. "I adapted
my corporate comedy set into my keynote called, 'How I Became
President of the United States,'" he told me. "It's a comedic, inspirational keynote that I performed around the world and people really loved."

Brown points to things in his background that informed
his view of Obama. "I was raised by a single white mom on the
south side of Chicago that was riddled with racism, and being
biracial, not even knowing what that oppression was at the
time, but not being able to swim in my grandma's pool and other
things that were still kind of segregated."

Brown worked several jobs in Chicago—as a model, wait-
er at a steakhouse, and as a reporter for a local TV station. He
began developing his Obama routine in 2008, assisted by Randy
Nolen, the promoter who had tremendous success orchestrating
Steve Bridges' career as a George W. Bush impersonator.

"Portraying Obama was a huge undertaking," says Brown.
"It's not like imitating Bush where you can go and just flub words
and say things that are incoherent and people laugh. I had to be
eloquent and act like the leader of the free world. I performed in
over 22 countries and met people in every walk of life, from the

poorest naked people on the streets of India to literally having a meeting with the billionaire on that same block in a high rise in India. Even though I made a good amount of money, I was able to have this life experience that I feel like I've lived 100 lifetimes already and done things that people only dream of, because of the character I represented."

◆ ◆ ◆

EVEN THE SECOND CITY TROUPE opted for a gentle, Vaughn Meader-style treatment of Obama in a 2009 review called "Barack Stars," performed at Washington's Woolly Mammoth Theater, a few blocks from the National Mall. The cast pulled no punches depicting Chief of Staff Rahm Emanuel's temper and Biden's proclivity for run-on sentences, but with Obama the material centered on how much people admire him...

> MAN: *Can Obama really turn Guantanamo into the next*
> *Six Flags?*
> CROWD: (Singing) *Yes he can. Yes he can!*
> MAN: *But can he really make smoking good for you?*
> CROWD: (Singing) *Yes he can. Yes he can!*

The Obama role was played by Sam Richardson—who three years later would break through in HBO's comedy "Veep" as the overly-earnest political aide Richard Splett. He studied Obama for over a year. "Sometimes when he speaks, he's got a little bit of Martin Luther King in his voice," Richardson told NPR. "So sometimes he'll, you know, go, 'Now, what we need to do as a people is come together and achieve what we can all achieve.'

"Because Obama's got so many nuances, and he's such a dynamic figure, it's fun to play with that."

◆ ◆ ◆

FEW ENTERTAINERS HAVE CAPTURED OBAMA as well as Keegan-Michael Key and Jordan Peele. "There was something in the zeitgeist amongst the comedy community," Key recounts. "He seems so graceful and so competent; what is it that we're supposed to do to lampoon him?" Though both were enthusiastic Obama supporters, they managed to drill down to a deeper level of understanding—first on Fox's "Mad TV" and then on their own Emmy-winning Comedy Central series "Key and Peele." (The show was originally designed as "Key Versus Peele," but the two buds couldn't find enough material about which they might even pretend to disagree.) They each do Obama, with slightly different intonations, but both with keen insight.

Peele was born to a white woman named Lucinda Williams, who raised him on Manhattan's Upper West Side, and a Black man, Hayward Peele, whom Jordan last saw when he was seven. Key, eight years Peele's senior, was born in Southfield, Michigan, to a white woman and Black man, who gave him up for adoption to a white woman, Patricia Walsh, and a Black man, Michael Key, both social workers.

Cast together on "Mad TV," Key and Peele took note of Obama's political ascent and were drawn to the similarities that his bi-racial background had with theirs. One of the duo's recurrent takes on Obama's character centers on behavior alteration known as code switching. "You adapt to the cultural environment that you are in at the moment," Key explained during an interview with the Kunhardt Film Foundation, referring to the way a person speaks and even modifies his movements. "I think once I saw Obama doing it, it put me in a position to go, oh it's

Speechwriter David Litt, center, reviews script with Key and Obama.

interesting, everybody does it." According to Key, Obama's "cultural trapeze act has been a treasure trove for our comedy." An
early example came in a skit Key says was based on actual video
of Obama meeting members of a basketball team in Oklahoma.
"The way he would greet the (Black) basketball players was different from the way he would greet the white coaching staff."
An even sharper version came in a sketch in which Peele portrayed Obama meeting fans after a speech. He's strictly cordial
with white admirers but shifts dramatically with Black constit-
uents—at one point hugging and kissing a Black woman's baby,
and then shaking hands with a white woman's infant daughter.

This two-Obamas concept was further exploited in recurrent sketches featuring Obama (Peele) and his anger translator Luther (Key). In an installment titled "Obama Loses His
Shit," the president delivers his weekly radio address and calmly
discusses world affairs, while Luther fumes in the background

Obama and "Luther" at the 2015 Correspondents' Dinner.

and delivers his rant: "I have a birth certificate! I have a hot-dig-gity-doggity mamase-mamasa-mamakusa birth certificate, you dumb-ass crackers!" (Obama praised the sketch during an appearance on "The Tonight Show.") Peele says the Luther routines were rooted in SNL's famous "Mastermind" piece in which Phil Hartman played two sorts of Reagans—one who is lame in public and the other who is a sharp manipulator in private. "That's informed a handful of scenes of ours," Peele explained. "It's a version of that."

"We called Luther an anger translator as opposed to an anger expresser," says Key, "because I think what's happening is we are translating emotionally what Obama's saying. So it's all subtext. He's speaking with this very cool, graceful erudition, and then you hear what his id is saying, what the raw emotion is saying. So you're translating it into anger."

Key and Peele were flat out gobsmacked when offered the

chance to meet Obama during a brief stop he made at a Los Angeles hotel. The president hugged both men and, from the perspective of someone with the weight of the world on his shoulders, said, "I know it's hard for a brother on TV." In April 2015, Key was invited to do his Luther character alongside Obama at the White House Correspondents' Dinner, in a five-minute routine written entirely by the president's staff. It was reminiscent of how Steve Bridges stood next to George W. Bush at the WHCD nine years earlier, channeling Bush's inner thoughts...

> OBAMA: *I'm a mellow sort of guy, and that's why I invited Luther, my anger translator, to join me here tonight.*
> [Key, stern, with eyes bulging, enters to huge applause.]
> LUTHER: *Hold on to your lily-white butts!*
> OBAMA: *In our fast-changing world, traditions like the White House Correspondents' Dinner are important.*
> LUTHER: *I mean, really, what is this dinner? And why am I required to come to it? Jeb Bush, do you really want to do this?*
> OBAMA: *Because despite our differences, we count on the press to shed light on the most important issues of the day.*
> LUTHER: *And we can count on Fox News to terrify old white people with some nonsense: Sharia law is coming to Cleveland. Run for the damn hills!*

The routine ends with Obama reversing roles, seeming to lose his temper, and Luther quitting on the spot. As he exits, Luther whispers to Michelle Obama, seated on the dais, "He crazy!"

◆ ◆ ◆

Key and Peele on Comedy Central.

CONSERVATIVE CRITICS COMPLAINED that impression-
ists went easy on Obama, with soft takes of the sort Jay Pharoah
delivered on SNL. Pharoah, meanwhile, expressed frustration
over restraints imposed by producers. "For the last year and a
half they did no Obama sketches at all," he said. "They just were
like, 'oh, we don't know what to do...' I said, 'just let me do my
characters and we'll be fine.' They didn't wanna do that."

Obama's presidency did prompt SNL to give more attention to other politicians. These secondary impersonations often stole the show—particularly in 2008 when Obama sought
the nomination versus Hillary Clinton (Amy Poehler) and, later, faced vice presidential opponent Sarah Palin (Tina Fey). The
sketches, made better by Fey's uncanny resemblance to the

Alaska governor ("I can see Russia from my house"), offered the show's most biting satire.

To whatever extent Obama was grateful for his treatment by SNL, he decided in the final weeks of his presidency to award the Medal of Freedom to the man who made it possible...

> *One of the most transformative entertainment figures of our time, Lorne Michaels followed his dreams to New York City, where he created a sketch show that brought satire, wits, and modern comedy to homes around the world. Under his meticulous command as executive producer, 'Saturday Night Live' has entertained audiences across generations, reflecting — and shaping — critical elements of our cultural, political, and national life. Lorne Michaels' creative legacy stretches into late-night television, sitcoms, and the big screen, making us laugh, challenging us to think, and raising the bar for those who follow. As one of his show's signature characters would say, "Well, isn't that special?"*
> —President Barack Obama

12 / *Lie about everything*

On a Friday afternoon in 2004, actor and impressionist John Di Domenico got an urgent call from his agent. "Can you do Donald Trump?" she asked. Di Domenico wasn't sure. He'd seen Trump on "The Apprentice," which had just wrapped its first season on NBC, and had played with the voice in his head. "Give me an hour," he replied. Soon he called back and said he was confident he could do it—then ran out and bought DVDs to study and spent the weekend practicing. On Monday Di Domenico was hired as a Trump impersonator. And the employer? Donald Trump himself.

The gig consisted of recording hours of dialogue to be used at Trump's Taj Mahal hotel in Atlantic City as part of a live game for guests called "The Boardroom." (Trump apparently balked at paying NBC a fee for the name "The Apprentice.") After entering the room, players were told that Trump had been detained elsewhere but was on the speakerphone—which was, in fact, the voice of John Di Domenico.

So began a long and lucrative career for Di Domenico as arguably the nation's best and busiest Trump impersonator.

IT'S HALLOWEEN!
YOUR GUIDE TO THE SCARY SEASON
PAGE 19

HIGH-GRADE SCANDAL
'A' IS THE NEW 'C' AT
ELITE L.A. SCHOOLS
PAGE 44

SOUR GRAPES
THE SKINNY ON
CELEBRITY WINES
PAGE 30

Los Angeles

ADVENTURES OF A
FAKE
PRESIDENT
WHAT'S IT LIKE TO SPEND A DECADE
AS DONALD TRUMP'S DOUBLE?
INSIDE THE SURREAL WORLD
OF POLITICAL IMPERSONATORS

✚

KAMALA HARRIS
LAYS DOWN THE LAW
PAGE 58

$5.95
OCTOBER 2020
LAMAG.COM

Di Domenico gains fame by becoming Trump.

Their paths kept crossing in unusual ways. Later in 2004 Trump did a TV commercial for Visa in which he accidentally drops his Visa card off the roof of Trump Tower. In the next scene Trump climbs into a dumpster on the street to retrieve the card. For this, filmmakers used a body double wearing a wig created by renowned Broadway hair and makeup artist Bob Kelly. After the shoot Di Domenico contacted Kelly, paid him $5,000 for the wig, and began creating an act in which he both looked and sounded like Trump. Meanwhile, the real Trump, always eager for a buck, was scheduled to appear on the morning program "Fox & Friends" to promote Embassy Suites hotels. When Trump found he couldn't make it, Di Domenico was hired to take his place. He was so convincing that the hosts had to assure viewers this was not the real Donald Trump.

"By the time the 2016 election came," Di Domenico told me, "I had done Trump hundreds and hundreds of times all over the country, even all over the world. So, when he announced his candidacy in June of 2015, if you Googled 'Trump impersonator' I was number one, just by sheer luck of having chosen to do him so many years before. As an actor-comedian, I have to tell you, I was in the right place at the right time."

◆ ◆ ◆

DI DOMENICO WAS BORN in the Philadelphia suburbs in 1962, just a few days before the release of Vaughn Meader's "The First Family" album. As a kid he watched Ed Sullivan on TV, his favorite performers being John Byner and David Frye, whose imitations he would replicate for neighbors. "I had a speech impediment," he explains, "but for some reason, when I would do voices I had no impediment." At age nine Di Domenico bought his first record album, Frye's "Richard Nixon: A Fantasy." He was captivated by the way Frye could tell an entire story through his impressions, rather than just mimic a voice. Moreover, he became interested in politics and later, while attending Temple University, interned for Pennsylvania Senator Arlen Specter.

During eight years of therapy to correct his speech impediment, Di Domenico was provided with what he calls a "tool kit" for breaking down speech patterns. After becoming a professional entertainer he used those tools to analyze the voices of people he would impersonate.

As someone who has studied Trump for decades, Di Domenico makes an intriguing observation. "When you watch early interviews he did with Tom Snyder and Oprah, he had this really large, impressive lexicon. His vocabulary was much bigger and he was less verbose." When Trump announced his candidacy in 2015, "his lexicon had shrunk dramatically. He was using very specific keywords. And I'm thinking, where did this come from? Who, in their seventies, starts adopting new phrases? And he started doing triplets, which he'd never done before. You know, 'I love, love, love...'"

You assume this is all intentional?

"One hundred percent. I can't imagine that it's not."

Over time Di Domenico gradually sharpened his criticism of Trump—even when portraying him for corporate groups, which he says almost always lean conservative. He also became so facile in ad-libbing as Trump that his in-character interview appearances were as focused as the carefully scripted material being offered elsewhere. An example...

> INTERVIEWER: *When is it okay to lie to your partner?*
> TRUMP (Di Domenico): *Right away. This is so import-ant, a great question. Start lying immediately, and this is why. Women are very tough about lying. Eventually, you're going to lie and your wife or girlfriend is going*

to say, 'You lied to me.' But if you've been lying all along,
you're covered. Somewhere along the line with a woman
you're going to get caught in a lie, so just lie right off
the bat, lie about everything. Lie about absolutely every-
thing. It's so important."

◆ ◆ ◆

RONALD REAGAN USED TO JOKE that he was just a humble actor cast in the role of president. At least Reagan recognized the humor in that. Donald Trump's persona, on the other hand, was so contrived and calculated that it raised the question: How do you impersonate a president who is, himself, impersonating a president? As Al Franken told me, "He's so vile as a human being and was so out of the norm in such a toxic way that it was impossible to find any good traits." Franken wasn't suggesting that searching for positives in Trump's character was requisite; rather, that without redeeming qualities the impersonations dwelled on obvious traits that both opponents and supporters knew well—and which, for different reasons, neither group found particularly funny.

Sophia McClennen, a professor at Penn State, has studied Trump and satirists' efforts to lampoon him. "Trump was already a celebrity," she notes, "so he was very unusual because he had celebrity identity that already had decades of jokes about it. There's a long history of this going back at least to the '80s." McClennen believes impressionists had to rummage in their toolkits to deal with Trump—at times trading a hammer for a mallet. "He was already an exaggeration. He was already absurd, like at a level we really hadn't had in a public figure, certainly since TV began."

Trump, for the most part, loved it. During the 2016 campaign he agreed to appear with Jimmy Fallon on "The Tonight Show" in a sketch that was inventive and well crafted, while confirming Trump's thirst for publicity. Madeup and dressed to look like Trump, Fallon had a "conversation" with his image in a dressing room mirror—with the part of the reflection played by the real Trump. Fallon said he was studying "my beautiful reflection," adding, "I'm like a Greek god who took a bath in a Pumpkin spice latte." Fallon did many more Trump sketches after the election but, as analyzed by McClennen, "Fallon's impersonation of Trump fell flat. He did the standard move of offering an exaggerated physical rendition of Trump, but that was boring since it captured neither Trump's bluster, nor his dangerous ineptitude, nor his bigoted, sexist, selfish nature."

One performer who sought to dig deeper was Anthony Atamanuik, a writer and actor who toured doing Trump for theater audiences and then in 2016 expanded the character in creating Comedy Central's "The President Show." As he defines it, "We wanted to package a really serious message about this man who clearly because of his mother complex and misogyny is a damaged individual who should not be anywhere near nuclear weapons."

Atamanuik's show frequently placed the Trump character in real life situations. One of the best occurred during the Tax Day event on April 15, 2017, when protesters showed up in more than 150 U.S. locations demanding that Trump release his tax returns. The organizers, including Maryland Congressman

Jamie Raskin and law professor Jennifer Taub, invited Comedy Central to do a bit during the Washington demonstration. With cameras shooting documentary style, Atamanuik arrived by limousine and joined the march to the Capitol. He mingled with actual protesters—leading to some very entertaining is-this-real? encounters...

WOMAN: *Why won't you release your taxes?*

TRUMP: *You don't know what I'm going to release, but it's going to be a full release when I do it. Haven't you ever been to a massage parlor?*

At another point, he wades into a crowd where signs such as "Despicable Trump" are held high. He spots an 8-year-old Black girl...

TRUMP: *What a wonderful little girl. Do you want to take a picture with me?*

GIRL: *You're a disgrace to the world!*

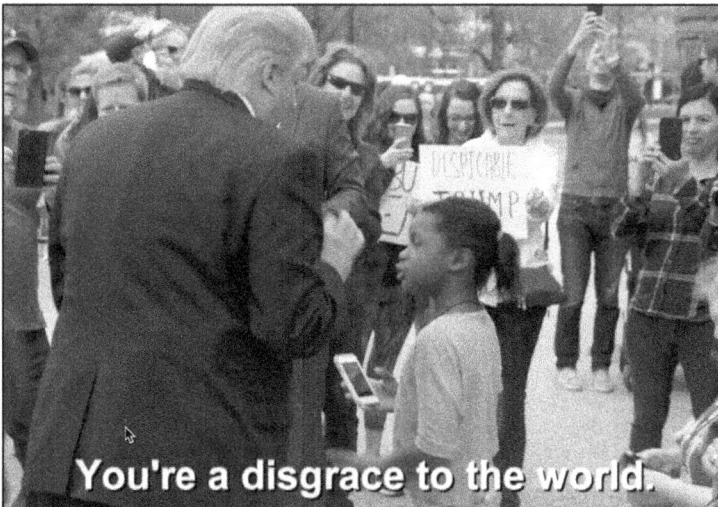

Youngster gives Atamanuik a piece of her mind.

"That was so awesome," Atamanuik recalls. "As soon as I knew we had an editable point, I broke character because I was like, 'Does she think I'm Trump?' I said, 'You know I'm not Trump, right?' And she said, 'Yeah, but you look like him and that's what I would say to him.' So I said to the father, 'You have a very wise daughter.'

"I couldn't believe the things people wrote later about a little Black girl. Disgraceful. It was the first time I realized how nasty people can be online."

What Atamanuik told me next was also a disgrace. A man he described as "wild-eyed" jumped the barrier and ran at him. Atamanuik was accompanied by two "Secret Service agents"— but they were actors, not prepared to deal with a real attacker. Fortunately Comedy Central had also hired guards from the renowned Gavin de Becker security firm, who wrestled the man to the ground.

At the conclusion of his routine, Atamanuik took the stage and addressed the crowd...

> TRUMP: *What's the big deal about releasing my tax returns? First of all, I claim Ivanka as three dependents: my daughter, my mother and my wife.*
> (Aides throw shredded paper to the crowd.)
> TRUMP: I *told Jared to shred my taxes. I thought shred was Yiddish for collate.*

Over the next year, as Atamanuik did more Trump routines in public, he found things became increasingly difficult. "Part of the issue," he explains, "was that people were getting more violent with me when I was out, throwing cans at me. So

Atamanuik portrays Trump on "The President Show."

there was sort of an event horizon, where I started to be like, they're not paying me enough for me to get hurt. We started doing more contrived scenes where maybe people in the background were real, but I was working with actors. We started to structure and control it a little bit more as the show progressed."

After two seasons the audience got smaller and the remaining viewers skewed older. "I think people got sick of the Trump humor," Atamanuik told me. "There was a lot of Trump fatigue."

◆ ◆ ◆

"SATURDAY NIGHT LIVE" has long loved the Trump character, stretching as far back as 1988 when Phil Hartman first played him. Jason Sudeikis tried the role once, Taran Killam three times, and Darrell Hammond 27 times over a 17-year stretch. Just before Trump was elected Alec Baldwin took over, playing Trump 46 times until 2020 when the job went to James Austin Johnson. Jim Downey, the renowned SNL writer, once called Hammond's Trump impression "the gold standard."

Hammond was rather cagey about his personal politics when I spoke with him. He had, at minimum, a tolerance for some aspects of Trump's character and personality. His first opportunity to study the man occurred in 2004 when Trump hosted SNL. "No one ever came earlier, no one ever stayed later. He converted unpleasant into pleasant," Hammond recalls, adding that he was especially taken by the way Trump interacted with kids Ivanka and Barron when they visited Studio 8H. "I don't hate Trump," Hammond once told the *Washington Post*. "Why would an anthropologist hate his work?"

In Trump's 2004 appearance he gets a huge ovation and begins his opening monologue with: "It's great to be here at 'Saturday Night Live' but I'll be completely honest, it's even better for 'Saturday Night Live' that I'm here. Nobody's bigger than me. Nobody's better than me. I'm a ratings machine." He introduces Hammond, who enters in character as Trump...

TRUMP: *Darrell, I love what you do. It's great. Do that thing. Go ahead.*
HAMMOND: *You're fired.*
TRUMP: *Do it again, Darrell. I love it.*
HAMMOND: *You're fired.*
TRUMP: *Keep firing, Darrell. We're going to clean out NBC.*

Trump was invited back to host SNL in November, 2015— a decision by Lorne Michaels that some viewers and critics considered inappropriate, since Trump had officially announced his candidacy five months earlier. However, the GOP field was crowded and Trump's campaign was widely regarded as laughable. He received substantial applause as he walked out, though not as robust as had been the case in 2004. "Many of the greats have hosted this show," he began, "like me in 2004. A lot of people are saying, 'Donald, you're the most amazing guy. You're brilliant. You're handsome. You're rich. You have everything going. The world is waiting for you to be president. So, why are you hosting Saturday Night Live? Why?' And the answer is, I have nothing really better to do."

He's joined on stage by Taran Killam and Darrell Hammond, both in full Trump makeup and attire, which now includes the long red tie...

> TRUMP (Killam): *You're doing a great job. In fact I think this show just got better by about two billion percent. In fact they just told me that now that I'm here this is the best monologue in SNL history!*
>
> TRUMP (Hammond): *You think you're this terrific person. You think you're this, you think you're that. Bup-bup-bah. You're being very naive and frankly, you're fired.*
>
> TRUMP: *They're great. They don't have my money, my talent or especially my good looks.*

Later in the show—and, remember, this was a full year before the 2016 election—a sketch titled "White House 2018" was remarkable. In a meeting with staff in the Oval Office, the real Trump learns that his MAGA programs are a big hit ("Everyone loves the new laws you tweeted").

ARMY GENERAL (Kenan Thompson): *ISIS is completely eliminated, sir. [Syria] is at peace. All the refugees have returned and they have great jobs as blackjack dealers at the Trump Hotel and Casino in Damascus.*

REAL TRUMP: *Madam Secretary, how's the situation in Russia?*

SECRETARY OF STATE (Sasheer Zamata): *Never better. After your face-to-face meeting, Putin has withdrawn from Ukraine. Believe me, he does not want to be called a loser again. He cried for hours.*

REAL TRUMP: *Well, I'm sorry. I just had to do that. Keep up the good work, Omarosa. ...*

MELANIA (Cecily Strong): *It's hard. This White House is the smallest place Donald and I have ever lived.*

AIDE: *Mister President, your daughter, the Secretary of the Interior, is here.*

REAL IVANKA TRUMP: (Regarding White House renovations) *The private swimming pool and cabanas are already completed. And now, if you'll excuse me, today we are covering the Washington Monument in gold, mirrored glass.*

ENRIQUE PEÑA NIETO (Beck Bennett): *I brought the check for the wall.*

REAL TRUMP: *That's so much. It's not going to cost me that much.*

EPN: *I insist. Consider it an apology for doubting you. As history shows us, nothing brings two countries together like a wall.*

REAL TRUMP: *Well, I told you you could do it. And I want to thank you for changing Telemundo to only English.*

Trump breaks the fourth wall and tells viewers, "If you think that's how it's going to be when I'm president, you're wrong. It's going to be even better. I said to the writers of this sketch, keep it modest, okay. It's better to start with low expectations. That way you have nowhere to go but up." Melania (Strong) steps forward to add, "So this election season, before you vote, dream. Dream of Melania for first lady." The announcer reads, "This message paid for by the Melania for First Lady Foundation, a Trump Organization corporation."

The sketch marked a turning point in how SNL and other entertainment media dealt with Trump. Though he didn't write the material, Trump controlled the message, confirming his political strength among a majority of Americans for whom no amount of satire would affect his image or support.

◆ ◆ ◆

AS THE 2016 ELECTION APPROACHED, game planning at "Saturday Night Live" seemed clear: After Hillary Clinton's victory she would be portrayed for at least four years by the multi-talented Kate McKinnon; loser Donald Trump would be played in the final weeks of the campaign, and periodically thereafter, by the equally skilled Darrell Hammond. But in late summer Hammond was told by producer Steve Higgins that the Trump role was being given to veteran actor Alec Baldwin. Hammond quotes Higgins as saying, "We're going to replace you as Trump. Alec is really famous, and you're not." Lorne Michaels, who made the decision to bring in Baldwin, told the *Washington Post*, "I needed another force, on an acting level, to have the power that Trump was embodying then. The Darrell Trump ... it wasn't the Trump that had gotten darker. It was the Trump from 'The Apprentice.'"

Hammond was sick—literally. After getting the word from Higgins he sat on his couch vomiting violently. He couldn't even bring himself to watch the returns on Election Night, opting for "Game of Thrones." Baldwin took over the role on October 1, 2016, on a night he recalls this way...

> *The stage manager took me to the edge of the stage ... and I stood there and I go, I don't know what I'm gonna do. I mean, we're about to do it. And I just remember, eyebrow down, eyebrow up ... masticate the words as much as you can. And get your mouth out as far. And really, really masticate the words ... and then the hands ... wax-on, wax-off. And you put together like three or four beats and then that's it. You just pick these three or four beats physically, and to me, I don't spend a lot of time thinking about what's going on inside him ... I see a guy who seems to pause, to dig for the more precise and better language that he wants to use and never finds it.*

Baldwin's first words on-air as Trump came in a faux debate: "Good evening, America. I am going to be so good tonight, I am going to be so calm and presidential, that all of you watching are going to cream your jeans."

That set the tone for the 46 times Baldwin would play Trump. He'd be portrayed as a pompous, egomaniacal clown—

but in a superficial way that failed to expose true evil in Trump's character and policies. Moreover, in the weeks prior to the 2016 election Hillary Clinton (Kate McKinnon) was depicted as almost equally clownish. As Colin Jost put it on "Weekend Update," the choice between Trump and Clinton, "is like choosing a phone. We don't want the iPhone 7 (Clinton) because it feels like it's being forced on us. Also, it's not necessarily an improvement. But we also don't want the Samsung Galaxy (Trump) which could explode at any minute."

Baldwin, son of a school teacher, grew up on Long Island. He's appeared on stage, screen and television and his career has been marked by well-publicized run-ins with photographers and fans, as well as a horrific incident in 2021 when a revolver he was holding during rehearsal on a movie set discharged, killing one crew member and wounding another.

Baldwin won an Emmy in 2017 for his portrayal of Trump but SNL vet Al Franken told me he saw room for improvement. "I feel like the ball was dropped with Trump," he said. "I would have written it differently." Franken says most of the Trump sketches lacked sophistication. Instead of identifying Trump's most egregious behavior, most impressionists focused on his humorous but relatively harmless traits—things that his supporters actually admired, or at least tolerated. Typical Baldwin lines…

…In Trump's America men work in two places, coal mines and Goldman Sachs.

…Obama Care is a disaster and I have a replacement plan, okay? I just read about it this week, it's a terrific plan, just great. It's called The Affordable Care Act.

Baldwin does Trump on SNL.

Trump was predictably thin-skinned, tweeting, "Alec Baldwin, whose dying mediocre career was saved by his terrible impersonation of me on SNL, now says playing me was agony. Alec, it was agony for those who were forced to watch. Bring back Darrell Hammond, funnier and a far greater talent!"

Once Trump was defeated in 2020, Baldwin stepped away from the role, for which he was reportedly being paid only scale ($1,400 per appearance). He was replaced by newcomer James Austin Johnson, whose Trump had more nuance. But Johnson was also cast as SNL's new Joe Biden—a character with whom the show, and most entertainment media, foundered, raising doubts about whether a deeply divided nation any longer had the interest, or stomach, for biting presidential parody.

13 / *No joke*

It's 1991. Pan Am files for bankruptcy. A gallon of gasoline costs $1.14. The Dow Jones average breaks 3,000. "Dances with Wolves" wins the Oscar for Best Picture. Future baseball great Mike Trout is born. And an 18-year Senate veteran from Delaware, Joe Biden, is impersonated for the first time on "Saturday Night Live."

The sketch mocked Senate confirmation hearings for Supreme Court nominee Clarence Thomas (played by Tim Meadows) and focused on assertions of sexual harassment by Anita Hill (Ellen Cleghorne). The role of Biden, chairman of the Judiciary Committee, was handled by Kevin Nealon, sporting an impressive array of hair plugs...

> BIDEN (Nealon): *Professor Hill, I want to thank you for your patience here today. You've shown remarkable courage throughout your testimony. It couldn't have been easy for you, or any of us, to sit here for the last seven hours and talk about penis size, or large-breasted women having sex with animals, or pubic hairs on soft drink cans, or oral sex, or the Black man's sexual prowess, or*

large-breasted women having sex with animals. But we appreciate your candor. And we hope we can reschedule you for another session tomorrow.

The hilarious sketch centered on the unbridled sexual curiosity of the all-male panel that included Edward Kennedy (Phil Hartman), Howell Heflin (Chris Farley), Strom Thurmond (Dana Carvey), Paul Simon (Al Franken) and Biden. The future president was a somewhat minor player; indeed, 16 years would pass before Joe Biden was again impersonated on SNL. Jason Sudeikis assumed the role in 2007, playing it a total of 22 times over 13 years.

After Joe Biden became vice president, his character remained relatively nondescript across most media, and it stayed that way even after he became president. Indeed, he's the least lampooned since Eisenhower—who, after all, didn't have to worry about late-night TV monologues on multiple channels, YouTube mashups or savaging sketches on SNL.

But here's the funny thing about President Biden: Politics aside, the guy is a genuinely amusing character, with plenty of comedic hooks. He's an occasionally confused octogenarian, sometimes frisky with facts and inclined to spend five minutes telling a one-minute story. When he dons the type of dark aviator glasses that looked good on Gen. Douglas MacArthur in WWII, Joe Biden is comedy gold. And yet, comedians don't rip him nearly as much as his supporters might fear and his opponents would wish.

So, what's the deal with that?

♦ ♦ ♦

OVER DRINKS at the Polo Lounge in Beverly Hills in late summer 2019, Lorne Michaels offered Dana Carvey the Biden role. "He joked that he needed me 'yesterday,'" recalls Carvey, who turned it down, not wanting to travel from the West Coast where he was busy with other projects. Moreover, Carvey was unsure how to handle Biden. "There's a lot of sensitivity around Biden among comedians and writers," he told me.

Carvey found that for a while after the election it was difficult to do any Biden material because audiences weren't receptive. "It's loosened up a bit," he says, "but it's still a hot oven and you're not sure you want to touch it."

In fall of 2019, Michaels gave the Biden role to actor Woody Harrelson, who made no attempt to sound like the candidate, but flashed an impressive set of false teeth while delivering a serviceable performance...

BIDEN (Harrelson): *I'm like plastic straws: I've been around forever, I've always worked, but now you're mad at me?*

Two weeks later, Harrelson's Biden was part of a "CNN Town Hall" on LGBTQ issues...

BIDEN: *The vast majority of people in America are not homophobic. They're just scared of gay people.*

And then there was a faux debate in February, 2020, with Jason Sudeikis temporarily back in the role...

MODERATOR: *Mr. Biden, you have 60 seconds.*

BIDEN: *What? The doctor told me I had six to eight months!*

That was three weeks before the South Carolina primary, after which the odds of Biden getting the nomination shot up dramatically, and the odds of Biden being seriously mocked by impressionists plunged. As with Obama, who comics were reluctant to cast in a negative light, Biden was shielded from harsh jokes—not so much out of reverence for him but because of fears that wounding Biden could help re-elect Trump.

On SNL, the Biden role went next to comedian John Mulaney for a single, uninspired performance, after which the pandemic interrupted the show's studio production. The global emergency, serious as it was, made things easier for Biden as well as for those tasked with impersonating him on television. Biden was spared the rigors of in-person campaigning and was seen primarily via carefully controlled Zoom appearances from his Delaware basement. SNL and other late-night shows went into quarantine, with limited opportunities to mount political sketches. For seven consecutive months in 2020 there were no Biden impersonations on SNL.

In October, with the election drawing near, comic Jim Carrey was cast as Biden, with Lorne Michaels telling *The New York Times*, "Jim is brilliant, and he cares deeply about the country and what's going on. He wants to have a voice in this. Every time he's done [SNL], he's always come through brilliantly, and I think what he will bring to this part will be stunning and possibly transcend comedy. Because we're in a period where comedy is only part of it."

However, Michaels' decision to cast Carrey was widely criticized, both creatively and politically. A writer at *Vanity Fair* declared, "SNL has a Jim Carrey problem," suggesting that Carrey's edgy characterization might doom Biden's chances.

Baldwin as Trump, Carrey as Biden and Rudolph as Harris on SNL.

I found Carrey's portrayal to be effective, exaggerating the character hooks much as Dana Carvey did with George H.W. Bush. Carrey appeared on six consecutive shows in fall of 2020, beginning with the first Biden-Trump debate, which SNL's announcer described as, "pretty fun to watch, as long as you don't live in America."

BIDEN (Carrey): *I've got the beginning of 46 thoughts. Now let's do this! I'm holding my bladder, let's get at her.*

Perhaps Carrey was too spry, projecting the physicality of a younger Biden rather than what the septuagenarian candidate had actually become. But at 6'2" and slender, with a narrow face, Carrey came across as a much more believable Biden than the six other performers who have played the part before and since on SNL. On the episode following the election...

BIDEN: *I've never felt so alive, which is ironic because I'm not that alive.*

Carrey benefited considerably by working alongside SNL veteran Maya Rudolph, who turned in a compelling performance as Vice President Kamala Harris...

HARRIS (Rudolph): *To all the little Black and brown girls watching right now, I just want to say this: The reason your mom is laughing so much tonight, is because she's drunk. And the reason she's crying is because she's drunk.*

Jim Carrey left SNL immediately after the election, offering a goodbye tweet: "Though my term was only meant to be 6 weeks, I was thrilled to be elected as your SNL President...comedy's highest call of duty. I would love to go forward knowing that Biden was the victor because I nailed that s***. But I am just one in a long line of proud, fighting SNL Bidens!"

The show hurriedly turned to cast member Alex Moffat as its new Biden, yielding an anodyne portrayal apparently designed to avoid controversy.

BIDEN (Moffat): *I'm like Colonel Sanders—every time you see me I'm a different guy. There's a good chance that this time next year, I'm going to be Mario Lopez.*

With Moffat as Biden, SNL entered a period of total confusion about how to handle a president who could be as clumsy as Gerald Ford and as forgetful as Ronald Reagan, at a time when the nation's view of politics and comedy was shifting. Moffat first played the role in December, 2020, after which three months passed before SNL's next Biden sketch—and that was it for the entire season.

By fall the role had been recast yet again, with newcomer

James Austin Johnson does his Biden.

James Austin Johnson, who had done credible work on the comedy circuit portraying Donald Trump, giving it a try. His Biden, however, proved flat and uninspired and, at age 32, even a wig and makeup failed to make him Bidenesque. The closest Johnson came to a funny line in his entire first season, amidst the pandemic, was...

> America, I'm here to tell you, there's one simple thing you can do to make this whole virus go away: Stop seeing "Spiderman."

Johnson spoke by phone several times with Dana Carvey, perhaps in search of the secret sauce that would boost his Biden impression. "We didn't talk at all about how to do Biden," Carvey recalls. "We just talked about finding writers to collaborate with, what it's like doing the show as the new guy, and the best place to get a tuna sandwich. No joke!"

Regardless, no counseling from Carvey would be of much use as SNL shied away from Biden sketches and preferred to use Johnson as Trump, even after Biden was in office. During Biden's first two years in office, he was portrayed in only eight sketches. By comparison, during Trump's first two years in office, Alec Baldwin impersonated him on SNL 21 times.

◆ ◆ ◆

JIMMY FALLON HAS HAD MODEST SUCCESS impersonating Biden on "The Tonight Show." Earlier, he'd done well playing Trump, so as soon as Biden took office, Fallon's staff put together a reel of his speeches. "I played it over and over," Fallon explained, "so I could practice things he does, little nuances, the way his voice is and the way he moves his hands. He does a lot of eye-wiping, and he often sounds like he just got over a cold." As for the character himself: "I think our take on Biden has been these stories that he has that relate to the subject that he's talking about, but sometimes the stories are too long and a little bizarre. You know, 'I knew a guy who used to be called Mississippi Jack, and he would climb up a flagpole and stand next to it horizontally and he would pretend he's a human flag and we would all go out and salute him.'"

Stephen Colbert also did some Biden on "The Late Show," although he skipped the full makeup and never really tried to alter his voice. His Biden consisted mainly of dark aviator glasses and quips such as...

> I've got bad news about the single-payer health plan. You see, my dog stepped on the keyboard. Long story short: Blue Cross owns all your organs. Bad dog! P.S. Naked the whole time, Jack. Buffin' it.

Colbert also brought on Dana Carvey to do the impres-

Stephen Colbert offers an understated Biden.

sion several times. Carvey's view was that for a while after the 2020 election many liberal comedians felt they were in a "vise grip," squeezed between their political views and desire to get laughs. "Has politics gotten so serious and so entrenched that we have something bigger than our jokes right now?" he asks. "Some comedy writers feel they can't do something that will sabotage their guy and let the bad guy get leverage. I don't think any of this is spoken out loud. It's just obvious."

Nevertheless, Carvey's gift for finding the comedic core of the presidents he impersonates makes him far and away the best at doing Biden. In full wig and makeup, he told "Late Show" viewers, "Words. They're like Republicans. They don't want to work with me, but I keep trying anyway."

Carvey describes his Biden as "like the alien who came off the spaceship in 'Close Encounters.'" A delicious sample...

Folks, come on folks, let's get real. I'm not kiddin' around here. We gotta do the thing. We did Barack. We did the deal. My dad, my dad, lost his job in Scranton. No joke. No joke, I'm not being a wise guy here. I said, 'Pops, why'd you lose it?' He said, 'Joey I did.' My mom said that's the cookie that crumbles. But here's the deal: Number one, the thing that they said. Number two, the two part. Folks, come on, I'm not kiddin' around. No rocket science. Come on now. Here's the deal. He knew, he told, he knew it floated. He told Bob Woodward, uh Joanne Woodward, he told Bob Redford. Excuse me, you know. But folks, I care. I care a lot. People are suffering and my mother said, "That's the way the cookie is in those, those places."

Carvey said a year into Biden's term he asked some of Stephen Colbert's writers at CBS, "If Biden was a Republican, do you think we would go at him harder?" The response was, "That's a really interesting question." Translation: Yes.

On Fox News Channel, Greg Gutfeld's nightly show emerged during Biden's term as an island of conservative comedy. ("President Biden visited a Baskin-Robbins this week, making history as the first customer to get a brain freeze before eating the ice cream.") The show frequently turns to comedian and author Tom Shillue, who previously appeared as a correspondent on "The Daily Show," for his biting Biden impression...

I know a lot about water pressure. I was a lifeguard, okay, so don't tell me. I defeated Corn Pop with nothing but a whistle and two hairy legs. ... I could probably do more pushups than you and all your cousins.

Among the more unusual Biden portrayals is one created by comedian Kyle Dunnigan using an assortment of digital tools to combine a distorted image of Biden's face with Dunnigan's well-tuned vocal impression. He uses the popular apps Face Swap and Perfect Video to deliver what he calls "creepy" on-screen images that work comedically because they're not literal. "I find the goofy Face Swap is just funnier," he told interviewer Max Raskin, "because when your brain has to work and then realize something is slightly off—it's not freed up to laugh. But when it's so ridiculous looking, almost cartoonish, you know this is a safe thing in some lizard part of your brain."

Using a tool called Snap Camera, Dunnigan can play several parts at once, such as a scene in which Biden appears to "discover" himself in the bathroom mirror...

BIDEN: *Hey, who are you?*

BIDEN'S REFLECTION: *I'm you, man, come on. It's me, Joey B.*

BIDEN: *How'd you get in here? This is a security beach.*

REFLECTION: *Look, I've got a surprise for you. Your name isn't Jarrack O'Biden, it's Barack O'Jiden.*

BIDEN: *Who sent you? Vice Pedia Clydia Harris?*

REFLECTION: *No, man. Look, you'd gotta get your ass* (unintelligible).

BIDEN: *Let's go behind the bleachers. No one's lookin'. Five and a quarter for a sniff-and-tuck. ... All I know is, if you don't vote for me, you ain't a China guy.*

And then there's Rich Little, who turned 84 the same month Joe Biden turned 80. Little is the only professional to have impersonated all 12 sitting presidents since Kennedy, serving as a White House court jester whenever a Republican was in office.

His Biden isn't as good as his earlier impressions and, moreover, there hasn't been much market for it. During Biden's first two years in office, the only TV platform for Little was Mike Huckabee's variety show. It was originally on Fox News Channel and then moved to Trinity Broadcasting Network, which describes itself as, "the largest Christian Television Network in the world committed to sending the message of hope and grace of Jesus to the world." In this setting, Little and Huckabee are comfortable making jokes about Biden, with Little claiming, "Even some of the liberals are laughing. They don't understand it but they're laughing."

During one visit to Huckabee's show, Little walked haltingly across the stage, exaggerating Biden's gait, and declared, "President Harris and I are working hard for you. We're doing the work of three people: Larry, Curly and Moe."

◆ ◆ ◆

PROMOTER RANDY NOLEN made a lot of money by grooming presidential impressionists for the corporate circuit along with advertising gigs and local TV appearances. Nolen's remarkable success with Steve Bridges as George W. Bush led to an Oval Office visit, a landmark appearance at the Correspondents' Dinner, and several million dollars in fees. Nolen also profited handsomely representing Tim Watters, who had the good fortune to both look and sound like Bill Clinton. And, Nolen helped launch the career of Reggie Brown, arguably the most spot-on Barack Obama mimic.

When Donald Trump was elected, Nolen signed veteran standup comedian Dave Burleigh for the part. Burleigh does reasonably good celebrity voice impressions—ranging from Jack Nicholson to Owen Wilson—but he looks nothing like Trump. So Nolen turned to makeup wizard Kevin Haney for silicone facial pieces which, along with a $10,000 wig and a $7,000 set of false teeth, transformed Burleigh into a serviceable simulation of Trump. "We did not play Trump as a buffoon," Nolen told me. "We were following the same formula that we developed with Steve Bridges in that it was goofy, silly, yet clever. And not disrespectful." Nolen, himself a conservative, felt this tone worked best with corporate clients, but with Trump the field quickly became crowded, as he proved to be history's most impersonated president.

As soon as Trump lost in 2020, Nolen and his team sprang into action and invested in a new set of facial appliances to transform Dave Burleigh into Joe Biden. However, unlike during the Trump years, there weren't many buyers for Biden impersonators—not on mainstream TV or on the corporate cir-

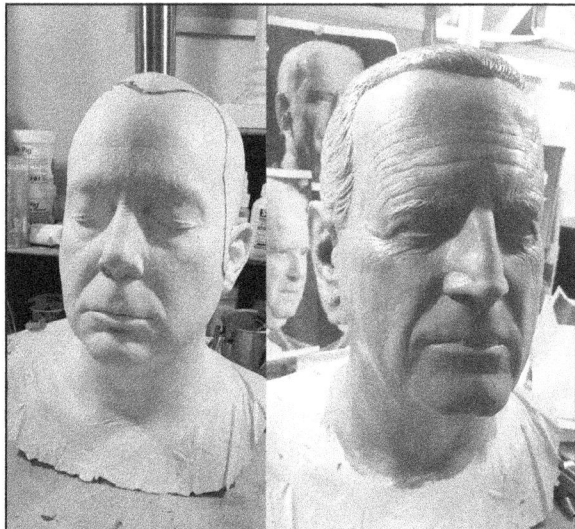

Artist Kevin Haney used a mold of Dave Burleigh's face, left, to create Biden facial appliances.

cuit. "I think the market is pretty savvy now," said Nolen. "They know what is good and what isn't good, because it's been done for the last 30 years."

In October 2021, Nolen arranged to have Burleigh test 15 minutes of his Biden routine at the Stand Up Comedy Club in Bellflower, a suburb of Los Angeles. Looking back, Nolen says makeup man Kevin Haney "had a bad day," and the Biden look was a bit off. "The chin was too large."

Nine months would pass before Burleigh's Biden act was ready for its official debut, at The Raven Room in Chicago. "The booker for the venue contacted us and practically begged us for dates," Nolen told me enthusiastically at the time. "With success on social media, a possible Netflix special, and a fall launch of the Biden project, Dave should be on his way." Instead, the two Chicago shows were canceled at the last minute due to poor ticket sales. There just wasn't much interest in Joe Biden—at least not as a comedy character. "I am certain it is because of the political 'angst' in Washington and around the country, and also the economy," Nolen reflected in an email. "With Steve Bridges as (George W. Bush) and Tim Watters as Bill Clinton, both parties were willing to have some fun. Even the Bush family liked Steve's portrayal and, as you know, we had a great relationship with them. Today, Democrats do not want to 'poke fun' at the boss and Republicans can't stand the guy."

At about the same time, another veteran promoter was also discovering that the Biden business was a bust. Denise Bella Vlasis, who runs Tribute Productions in LA (and does a slick Madonna routine herself), had been grooming comedian Gary Bley to impersonate Biden. One of her biggest clients, the conservative Young Presidents Organization, seemed eager, having had success with a Trump impersonator at a prior convention, and in 2021 Vlasis assumed Biden would be in demand. Instead, the group asked for actors to play Barack Obama, Vladimir Putin and Kim Jong-un. Then, with little notice, they canceled all of them and hired a music group for the night's entertainment. "There just doesn't seem to be much appetite for politics," Vlasis explained. "People used to laugh at politics, now everyone is touchy. I've been in this business for 40 years and I've never seen such a slump in interest in political entertainers."

♦ ♦ ♦

BACK IN 1975 PRESIDENT FORD slipped on the steps of Air Force One and Chevy Chase built his entire Ford character around it. In 2021, President Biden slipped on the steps of Air Force One and impressionists looked the other way.

When Joe Biden says "no joke," he might very well be describing his impact on presidential mimicry.

14 | *Making impressions*

I f you are impersonating a president, then you are speaking to the world," Jay Pharoah noted during our interview. "They're going to put that person and the character that you're portraying right beside each other."

In researching I sought feedback on two key questions: Do impersonations of presidents affect public perception and potentially influence voting? Has that changed significantly over the past six decades?

In his book, "Spoken Word: Postwar American Phonograph Cultures," Jacob Smith, a professor at Northwestern University, looks at the earliest mimics dating back to FDR and writes, "Imitative performance can retroactively define the subject of an imitation as an original. That is, when we see a person's action as imitation, we subtly ratify who was imitated as authentic. Here, then, is one reason for the White House's cautious embrace of presidential mimics, from the 1940s to the present day."

As we've seen, the genre emerged along with television in the early sixties and has evolved since Kennedy's presidency. JFK took office at age 43, handsome and charismatic, with a glamorous wife and charming kids. This was as close as Americans had ever come to having royalty in the White House, and Vaughn Meader's "The First Family" served to reinforce it. Thus, the first president to be widely depicted through impersonations while in office wasn't portrayed negatively, as was the case in years to follow; the genre actually emerged with a positive spin, almost the equivalent of a public relations campaign.

The next three presidents, however, endured harsh treatment and each paid a price. Johnson, Nixon and Ford were lampooned by impressionists and Ford, in particular, was victimized by the inaccurate depiction of him as a klutz. Chevy Chase declined to discuss it with me, but back in 2008 he spoke pointedly about the Ford era in an interview with CNN's Alina Cho...

CHASE: *I just went after him. And I certainly, obviously my leanings were Democratic and I wanted Carter in and I wanted [Ford] out and I figured look, we're reaching millions of people every weekend, why not do it.*

CHO: *You mean to tell me in the back of your mind you were thinking, hey I want Carter—*

CHASE: *Oh, yeah.*

CHO: *And I'm going to make him look bad.*

CHASE: *Oh yeah. ...*

CHO: *I talked to one political pundit who said, "I think Chevy Chase cost Ford the presidency."*

CHASE: *When you have that kind of a venue and power where you can reach so many millions of people ... you can affect a lot of people, and humor does it beautifully, because humor is perspective and has a way of making judgment calls. ... So I think there was no question that it had a major effect and in fact, in speaking with his family and then later him, and even reading some of his books ... he felt so, too.*

Chase wasn't the only impressionist to acknowledge having a political objective. David Frye's depictions of Johnson were laced with contempt—if not for the man himself then certainly for his policies. Harry Shearer used mimicry to remind Americans what a skunk Nixon was. John Roarke played Reagan as a greedy conservative. Improv groups such as The Committee and Second City, stage productions mounted by Garry Trudeau and Barbara Garson, and early television series including "TW3," "The Smothers Brothers" and "Fridays," all had stated goals to affect public opinion via political humor. Since the 1990s, however, impressionists have tended to be more circumspect—except during Trump's reign, when contempt for the man among most performers was hardly a secret. "I don't hate him," Alec Baldwin told *The New York Times* in 2017, "I want him to enjoy his life. I just want him to not be the president of the United States—as quickly as possible."

We like to think that comedic expression has expanded right along with the burgeoning media worlds of streaming and social media. With some topics it has, but presidential humor is more scattershot today than it was when the Smothers Brothers slammed Johnson, when SNL savaged Ford and when "Fridays" skewered Reagan.

◆ ◆ ◆

AMERICA'S MEDIA ARE AS DIVIDED as its politics. Conservatives dominate talk radio and maintain a powerful presence in cable-TV news, while liberals are the kings of comedy. So it makes sense that impressionists have tended to go easy on Obama and Biden, while doubling down on Trump.

"It's an incendiary time with politics, and that infiltrates political comedy," notes Dana Carvey. "With social media there's been more entrenchment, and people on both sides getting more angry. We all know that's going on. And so you tend to lose your sense of humor."

Lorne Michaels once expressed the belief that Republicans are easier to mock because they can take a joke, while Democrats tend to take everything personally. George W. Bush's reputation was unquestionably altered by Will Ferrell's "strategery" impression, but he tried to turn it to his advantage. Journalist Ron Suskind reported that Bush's team created the department of "Strategery," or the "Strategery Group," which meant "the oversight of any activity—from substantive policy to ideological stance to public event—by the president's political thinkers."

On the other hand, "The weight of the world is on a progressive," says Carvey, "because they're just more serious. Everything is an existential threat—climate change, existential threat Trump—and they are a little more serious about it."

In Rich Little's view, "I think I have some effect on an audience. When I do Biden and show him kind of out to lunch, it puts it in the back of your mind that, yeah, I guess he is that way." Darrell Hammond observes, "People today feel okay laughing at character-driven stuff—they feel like they don't have to choose sides as a Democrat or Republican."

Will Sasso, whose Clinton impersonation on "Mad TV" went closer to the edge than material on SNL, believes, "Politics is already a dirty game. So I don't think a sketch show is changing anything. The sketch is just mirroring what's happening. It's late on Saturday night, with mostly young people watching. I'd be shocked if it swayed people's votes."

The echo chamber effect in media applies to comedy just as it does to political news coverage. Nowadays viewers tend to support material that reinforces their beliefs, while tuning out the other side. Jimmy Kimmel says he lost half his audience as a result of his barrage of jokes against Trump. "Ten years ago, among Republicans, I was the most popular talk show host according to the research," he recounted on the podcast "Naked Lunch." Kimmel felt he had no choice but to stay true to his convictions, even after ABC executives asked him to dial it back. In today's entertainment world, he says, "There is a sacrifice you make when it comes to your audience." This division was further underscored at NBC, when Jimmy Fallon's "Tonight Show" lost viewers amid complaints that the host was being too gentle with Trump.

The current media mindset was driven home for me personally when "Playing POTUS" was pitched in Hollywood as a docu-series. Several potential buyers at major streaming services expressed a preference that the TV version of this book should remain "politically agnostic," so as not to offend viewers on either side of the aisle.

"There's a degree of 'this is what my audience wants,'" notes Robert Smigel, the veteran SNL writer. "It's kind of a reinforcing cycle for a loyal audience of people who agree with you.

After all, the people who don't aren't going to watch anyway.

"The expression POV (point of view) never really existed in comedy until somewhere in the nineties. Now we've sort of moved all the way in that direction. A lot of comedy is all about POV."

◆ ◆ ◆

SOME OF RECENT HISTORY'S MOST influential political impressions have involved presidential candidates, rather than the office holder himself. SNL drew this into focus by pioneering debate sketches that yielded some of the show's most memorable moments and allowed development of secondary characters, including women. In some cases these pre-election portrayals had a significant impact because candidates were less well known and voters were forming opinions about them in advance of an election.

A notable also-ran on SNL was Al Gore, the former vice president who faced George W. Bush in 2000. So powerful was Darrell Hammond's depiction of Gore in fake debates that his aides showed him tapes of the sketches so he could correct elements of behavior that were hurting his campaign.

Political scientists also cite the 2008 election in analyzing the impact of comedic impressions. They've even given it a name, the Fey Effect, referring to Tina Fey's devastating depiction of vice presidential candidate Sarah Palin. "There's no question that the impersonations were meant to make Palin not look electable," says Penn State's Sophia McClennen. Researchers at East Carolina University found that Palin's favorability, particularly among independents and Republicans, declined after the

SNL sketches. Moreover, the Fey Effect had a negative impact on Palin's running mate, Sen. John McCain. "Unlike negative political ads," they write in Public Opinion Quarterly, "political humor seems to be fairly popular, which could increase receptiveness to the message. And, because political humor is a form of negative priming, it should also be associated with more negative perceptions of its targets, particularly targets that are new to the national political scene."

◆ ◆ ◆

TODAY'S SMALLER, DIVIDED AUDIENCES blunt the impact of comedians and impressionists. Kennedy, Johnson, Nixon and Ford had their presidencies affected by comedic portrayals at a time when television options were limited—there was no cable-TV or streaming—and when Americans were more willing to accept humor regardless of the political party at which it was directed. Yet even in today's fractionalized media environment, impressionists do make an impression.

Prof. McClennen told me, "In general, the artists themselves, the creative side, almost invariably downplay any possible impact." Indeed, Darrell Hammond spoke for many impressionists when he explained, "I was trying to be funny, not to make a point." Yet, McClennen is convinced that, "They'll almost certainly have an effect. The question is what? Remember, the art of impersonation is that you're seeing something you haven't seen. The other thing, especially about a president, is that you're impersonating someone with substantial power. So the impersonation gives you an inside look at things people weren't supposed to see, adding to the sense of intimacy by filling in spaces.

And no matter what is being filled in, it's going to change how people think about the person being impersonated."

McClennen, like others who have analyzed humor in politics, points to two notable cases involving SNL: Chase's destruction of President Ford and Fey's searing portrayal of Palin. More subtle but equally significant, McClennen believes, is what occurred after 9/11 with impressions of George W. Bush. Whereas jokes about his intelligence initially seemed harmless, after the attacks such depictions had what she terms, "a major possibility of impacting public opinion about whether or not he should be leading the country in a moment of crisis."

The outlier among presidents in the Age of Impersonation is Trump. An untamed wig, orange makeup and an overly-long red tie were all it took for hundreds of Trump impersonators to work shopping malls, corporate events, Vegas stages and, of course, TV programs. He triggered countless parodies across a wide spectrum, but did it change public opinion?

"Trump engaged with Alec Baldwin repeatedly over the impersonations (on SNL)," says McClennen. "It was an historic first, and it happened in public on Twitter. This is the first time where you have an impersonation that is getting under the skin of the president, and the president is allowing his dislike of the impersonation to circulate broadly in the public sphere. The biggest impact of Baldwin may not have been the specific features of the impersonation, it was that Trump was so visibly bothered by them." Among his tweets:

> @NBCNews is bad but Saturday Night Live is the worst
> of NBC. Not funny, cast is terrible, always a complete hit

job. Really bad television! ...
Just tried watching Saturday Night Live—unwatchable!
Totally biased, not funny and the Baldwin impersonation
just can't get any worse. Sad.

McClennen believes Twitter records provide a useful measure of opinion during the period. "For the most part," she says, "the responses—and they're somewhat extraordinary in terms of their volume—were to regularly think that Baldwin was making Trump seem like a petulant child, and that he should focus on trying to lead the country, rather than worry about what was happening on SNL." It's worth noting that Twitter users and SNL viewers don't represent the nation as a whole.

According to a *New York Times* report, "After the election, Mr. Baldwin recalled, he was distressed to receive an email from a friend sardonically thanking him for humanizing Mr. Trump and helping him win.

"'I do recognize that that is a possibility,' Mr. Baldwin said. 'But I think that now that he is the president, we have an obligation—as we would if it was him or [Hillary Clinton]—to dial it up as much as we can.'"

Amy Becker, a communications professor at Loyola University, has studied this and reached conclusions quite different from those of Sophia McClennen. "By tweeting his critical response to SNL," she writes, "Trump presented viewers with another side of the story, engaging them with two-sided messaging. Rather than take the critical message about Trump's character and his fitness for the office of the presidency present in the SNL satire to heart, viewing Trump's Twitter criticism that the show was biased actually inoculated viewers against absorbing what SNL was saying."

Her research goes further, suggesting that rather than hurting Trump, Baldwin's portrayal might have damaged Democrats. In test groups, adjusted based on political leanings, it was shown that respondents actually lowered their opinions of Democrats Hillary Clinton and Tim Kaine after watching an SNL sketch about Trump and reading his pushback. "Ultimately," she concludes, "it appears that when coupled with his Twitter response, SNL was helping—rather than hurting—Trump."

Going forward Becker believes political comedy can't be evaluated in a vacuum. The full context across the spectrum of social media must be taken into account. In what she calls "our new period of disruption," analysts must consider, "the impact not just of comedy alone, but also the potential response to comedy across multiple media platforms."

◆ ◆ ◆

IT'S REASONABLE TO FEAR THAT the increasing volume of presidential impersonations diminishes the office as a whole, and the presidency itself becomes a joke. Regardless, the nation needs such parodies. Upon the release of "The First Family" album, the anthropologist Margart Mead observed, "This making fun of people in authority is very healthy. It is the difference between democracy and tyranny."

"We're supposed to question authority," says Dana Carvey. "I'm from the '60s and '70s, and that was the bumper sticker I had. A president is given massive power and authority, so it's our duty as the Brits would say, to 'take the piss out of 'em.'

"A president's primary job is to sell his agenda and sell his policies. They all shade the truth or exaggerate, every single one of them, because they're out there selling. So, therefore, all presidents are funny."

That's a pretty good punchline. It will be interesting to see how impressionists treat future presidents—particularly when the first woman is elected.

Regardless, no matter who occupies the White House, imitation will remain the sincerest form of comedy.

Notes

Many of the clips referenced are available on YouTube and other platforms. We've compiled the links and posted them along with other background material at:

http://www.PlayingPOTUS.com

Special thanks to Brian Courrejou for years of research. I'm also grateful for editing help and creative support provided by Amy Funt, Danny Funt, Clarence Fanto and Ken Oxman.

Additional thanks to Mike Shatzkin and Mark Itkin.

Cover art: Howard McWilliam.

Photo credits: Pg 27, Abbie Rowe, National Park Service, John F. Kennedy Presidential Library and Museum

Pg 28, Cecil Stoughton, White House, John F. Kennedy Presidential Library and Museum

Pg 40, 41, courtesy Bob Booker

Pg 55, courtesy Alan Myerson

Pg 68, courtesy Ruth Welch

Pg 76, courtesy Nixon Library

Pg 91, courtesy Alan Zweibel

Pg 96, courtesy Gerald R. Ford Presidential Library

Pg 115, 120, courtesy Ronald Reagan Library

Pg 123, courtesy Carson Entertainment Group

Pg 125, courtesy John Roarke

Pg 133, 149 courtesy George H.W. Bush Presidential Library and Museum

Pg 137, courtesy Dana Carvey

Pg 143, 151 courtesy Jim Morris

Pg 163, courtesy William J. Clinton Presidential Library

Pg 173, 231, courtesy Randy Nolen

Pg 177, photo by Kimberlee Hewitt, Courtesy
George W. Bush Presidential Library

Pg 193, courtesy Jay Pharoah

Pg 194, courtesy Reggie Brown

Pg 198, 199, photos by Lawrence Jackson, the White
House, courtesy Barack Obama Presidential
Library

Pg 211, photo by Deborah Feingold, courtesy
HarperCollins

Index

Also by Peter Funt . . .

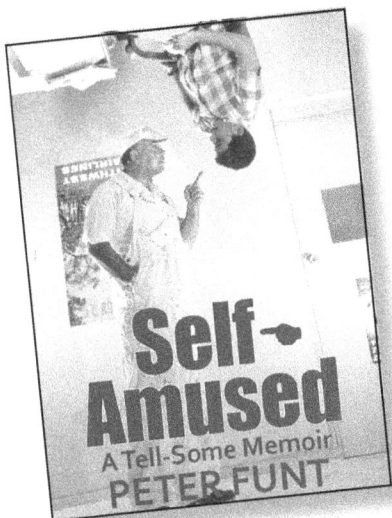

Self-Amused
A Tell-Some Memoir
PETER FUNT

"Peter Funt's collection of stories, memories and misfit adventures is insightful, hilarious, and just plain fun. I loved following Peter's journey. I'm honored to be part of it!"
—*Mayim Bialik*

In this collection of essays, Peter Funt examines our world with an eye toward major issues as well as those little things that sometimes drive us crazy.

THE DAILY BUGLE
CAUTIOUSLY OPTIMISTIC
Essays Across the American Landscape
—By PETER FUNT—

www.ingramcontent.com/pod-product-compliance
Lightning Source LLC
Chambersburg PA
CBHW031120020426
42333CB00012B/164